The Importance of Being
IDLE

The Importance of Being
IDLE

A LITTLE BOOK OF
LAZY INSPIRATION

Stephen Robins

PRION

This paperback edition published 2001
Reprinted 2002

First published 2000 by
Prion Books Limited
Imperial Works, Perren Street
London NW5 3ED
www.prionbooks.com

Text copyright © 2000 Stephen Robins
Design copyright © 2000 Prion Books

ISBN 1-85375-438-2

A catalogue record of this book can be obtained from the
British Library

Grateful acknowledgement is made to the following for permission to
reprint extracts from copyright material: *Enemies of Promise* by Cyril Connolly,
reproduced with permission of Andre Deutsch. Copyright © Cyril Connolly
1938. *Facts and Fancies* by Armando Iannucci, reproduced with permission of
(Michael Joseph) Penguin Books Ltd. Copyright © Armando Iannucci 1997.
The Importance of Living by Lin Yutang, reproduced with permission of Curtis
Brown Ltd, London, on behalf of the Estate of Mrs Lin Yutang. Copyright
© Lin Yutang 1938.

Cover design by Jamie Keenan
Printed and bound in Great Britain
by Creative Print & Design Ltd., South Wales

CONTENTS

INTRODUCTION

A

Achievement – Action – Akrasia – Afternoon Tea
Amateurs – Ambition – Ancient Greece – Armchairs

B

Bartelby the Scrivener – Beau Brummell – Beds
Breakfast – Brooke, Sir Basil Stanlake – Buchanites
Buddhism – Business – Busy Bees – Busy Idleness

C

Careerists – Chalmers, Thomas – Christianity
Civilisation – Clothes – Coleridge, Samuel Taylor
Contemplation – Creativity – Crime – Curiosity

D

Death – Dickens, Charles – Doing Nothing

E

Eichendorff, Joseph Von – Employment – Endymion
Energy – Evolution: the development of the human
brain – Excuses

F

Ford, Henry – Freedom

G

Getting out of Bed – Greek Philosophy
Goring, Lord

H

Happiness – Hard Work – Health – Heaven
Herodotus – History – Holidays – Housework
Hypochondria

I

Identity – Idleness – Idlers – Imagination
Indolence – Industry – Intellectuals – Inventiveness

J

Jerome K. Jerome – Johnson, Samuel

K

Kenko Yoshida

L

Lafargue, Paul – Laziness – Leisure – Letters – Life
Lin Yutang – Literature – Loafing – Lotus-Eaters
Love – Lying In Bed

M

Mankind – Marriage – Melancholy – Monasticism
Money – More, Sir Thomas

N

Nobility

O

Oblomov – Obligations

P

Paradise – Parliament – Patriotism – Plans – Play
Philosophy – Poetry – Protestant Work Ethic

Q

Quin, Gilbert

R

Relaxation – Retirement – Revolution – Rights
Rip Van Winkle – Rochester, Lord – Routine
Russell, Bertrand

S

Saki – Science – Seneca – Seven Deadly Sins – Seven
Sleepers of Ephesus – Sex – Shangri-La – Skelton,
John – Sleep – Sloth – Sluggards – Social Trends
Socialism – Somnus – Stevenson, Robert Louis
Stress – Success – Sunbathing
Suppression of Idleness

T

Technology – Time – Tobacco – Tramps – Truancy
Twain, Mark

V

Veblen, Thorstein

W

Weariness – Whitman, Walt – Wilde, Oscar
Wisdom – Work – Workaholics – The World

Y

Youth

INDEX
224

INTRODUCTION

The majority of Englishmen and Americans have no life but in their work; that alone stands between them and ennui ... they are too deficient in senses to enjoy mere existence in repose; and scarcely any pleasure or amusement is pleasure or amusement to them.

JOHN STUART MILL, 1848

A visitor ambling through the beautiful woods of Ferney complimented Voltaire on the astonishing growth of his trees. 'This should not surprise you,' Voltaire replied, 'for they have nothing else to do'. And with this, Voltaire strolled on, smiling to himself at the wisdom of his remark. This charming anecdote encapsulates the essence of this book. My claim, quite simply, is that idleness is good. It is good in itself: extended periods of languid indolence must be awarded prime positions in any sensible way of life. Moreover, the by-products of idleness are supremely good. Idleness leads to contemplation, creativity, and inventiveness, which, in turn, resolve themselves in literature, philosophy, poetry, and every other component of 'civilisation' as we know it. Idleness makes us – akin to Voltaire's trees – reach great heights without even trying.

It is a puzzling fact of modern life, then, that the adjectives 'idle' and 'lazy' are used as terms of censure rather than as terms of praise. The noun 'layabout' is used only in its pejorative sense as a term of condemnation, often preceded by the adjectival construct 'good-for-nothing'. Idleness is not recognised as a noble attribute or a virtuous pass-time.

The importance of being idle is ignored in most Western nations today, and has been for many centuries past, to the great disadvantage of these realms and the impoverishment of their respective cultural lives. This disastrous state of affairs must be remedied before it is too late. If idleness is vanquished by the pernicious cult of Hard Work, our lives will be forever dull. Most of us do not realise just how harmful work is. Work will damage your physical and mental health. Yet the stark fact of financial necessity ensures that we all have to work.

Hard work might make you richer in pecuniary terms, but it will invariably rob you of your passion for life and destroy your creative itch, leaving behind nothing but the burnt-out shell of your former self. Hard work will leave you culturally impoverished, spiritually indigent, destitute of true civilisation. We must do away with the exhausting Work Ethic before the spark of vitality is irreparably extinguished from our lives. We must kill work before work kills us. It is time to fight back.

You hold in your hands the first offensive, the first blast of the trumpet against the monstrous Work Ethic.

Every book, as Disraeli once told Metternich, is a battle lost or won. With the pen as my sword, it is time to march to the sound of drums. I aim to make clear the true benefits of sitting around all day doing absolutely nothing whatsoever. I aim to expose the destructive drudgery of the daily grind. This book marks the inauguration of this glorious revolution – the anti-work revolution, forever nurtured in the minds of the armchair revolutionaries.

ACHIEVEMENT

If a great thing can be done at all, it can be done easily. But it is that kind of ease with which a tree blossoms after long years of gathering strength.

JOHN RUSKIN

✪

The idler, who habituates himself to be satisfied with what he can most easily obtain, not only escapes labours which are often fruitless, but sometimes succeeds better than those who despise all that is within their reach and think every thing more valuable as it is harder to be acquired.

SAMUEL JOHNSON

✪

We do not know today whether we are busy or idle. In times when we thought ourselves indolent, we have afterwards discovered, that much was accomplished, and much was begun in us. All our days are so unprofitable while they pass, that 'tis wonderful where or when we ever got anything of this which we call wisdom, poetry, virtue.

RALPH WALDO EMERSON

WE WERE SITTING IN MY STUDY LATE one winter's afternoon, drinking cognac and discussing whether greatness is simply ephemeral fame under the pretence of perpetuity. Half a bottle later, we were still dissecting greatness and anatomising success. Sobriety has never generated such splendid conversation.

'We must not measure success by achievement,' I said, standing up cautiously to look through the window at the world outside. It was beginning to get dark already. 'The authentic idler,' I continued, 'will never measure success by achievement.'

'How very unwise of him,' my companion interjected. 'Intelligent men should always appreciate great achievements. Enlightenment is the only difference between us and the ignorant masses.'

'Certainly the idler might admire other men's achievements,' I replied, sitting down again, 'but he will do so from afar, and he will never make a conscious effort to emulate them. He will not exert himself on account of any particular goal. Such goals are never fixed in his sights.'

'The man who refuses to aim at excellence will never achieve greatness,' my friend said abruptly, reaching for his glass of cognac. 'The idler's existence, therefore, will be debased by the uninspiring mediocrity of the unambitious. In life, one must set one's sights as high as possible in order to succeed.'

'You misunderstand,' I retorted. 'The idler will achieve greatness accidentally. For him, achievements are simply the unexpected things that happen, as if by magic, when life takes its unpredictable and meandering path. All momentous discoveries have been unintentional.'

'Prove it,' he demanded.

'Look at Newton's discovery of gravity for example,' I said, leaning back into the comfortable depths of my armchair. 'There he was, snoozing under an apple tree one sunny day, when an over-ripe fruit detached itself from the branch and fell on his head. He woke with a disconcerted yelp. But as he realised what had happened, everything suddenly clicked into place, and the law of gravity was discovered.'

'Hurrah for the law of gravity, and three cheers for idleness,' announced my friend, with the dry insouciance of an apathetic dandy.

One must start out with a belief that there are no catastrophes in this world, and that, besides the noble art of getting things done, there is a nobler art of leaving things undone.

LIN YUTANG

☞ AMBITION
AMATEURS
CAREERISTS

ACTION

An inability to stay quiet, an irritable desire to act directly, is one of the most conspicuous failings of mankind.

WALTER BAGEHOT

✪

Act if you like – but do it at your peril. Men's actions are too strong for them. Show me a man who has acted, and who has not been the victim and slave of his action.

RALPH WALDO EMERSON

✪

To do nothing is the wisdom of those who have seen fools perish.

GEORGE MEREDITH

AKRASIA

Akrasia was a term used by Greek philosophers when discussing a form of moral idleness. It translates literally as 'bad mixture', but it was used by these philosophers to describe a character trait which modern scholars translate as 'weakness of the will'. This condition is one in which a man is unable to perform actions that are known to be right. Socrates argued that doing good follows from knowing what is good, but Aristotle maintained that human behaviour is often "akratic". Aristotle's view is the more persuasive. We often know that we should do something morally commendable, but we simply can't be bothered. Akrasia is the moral equivalent of knowing that you want a cup of tea but being too lazy to get up and make it.

☞   GREEK PHILOSOPHY

AFTERNOON TEA

There is something in the nature of tea that leads us into a world of quiet contemplation of life.

LIN YUTANG

✪

There are few hours in life more agreeable than the hour dedicated to the ceremony known as afternoon tea.

HENRY JAMES

✪

Tea, though ridiculed by those who are naturally coarse in their sensibilities, will always be the favourite beverage of the intellectual.

THOMAS DE QUINCEY

There is something extraordinarily enchanting about the English tradition of afternoon tea. The very words conjure up romantic visions of colonial types relaxing on the veranda, sipping fragrant Earl Grey from fine china cups, or English gentlemen watching cricket and nibbling gently on dainty cucumber sandwiches.

Of course, afternoon tea is a peculiarly English ritual. The nearest foreign equivalent is the siesta, an idea rooted in the same desire to bring the day to a complete standstill in mid-afternoon. When the Spaniard goes back to bed, the Englishman takes his tea.

Afternoon tea provides an essential period of rest and recuperation for the man wearied by a heavy luncheon. It is a time to ruminate on the happenings of the day so far, a time to sit back and take a well-earned break.

AMATEURS

In a world where no one is compelled to work more than four hours a day, every person possessed of scientific curiosity will be able to indulge it, and every painter will be able to paint without starving, however excellent his pictures may be. Young writers will not be obliged to draw attention to themselves by sensational pot-boilers, with a view to acquiring the economic independence needed for monumental works, for which, when the time at last comes, they will have lost the taste and capacity.

BERTRAND RUSSELL

✪

Under a system of permanent revelry, we will witness the Golden Age of the dilettante which will put the Renaissance to shame.

BOB BLACK

The idler is – by definition – an amateur. His few pastimes are pursued sporadically, and at a leisurely pace, as a source of pleasure. His time is spent exactly as he chooses. He feels nauseous at the mere whiff of professionalism, for a simple diversion is transformed into a compulsory and cheerless chore if pursued professionally. Instantly it becomes obligatory and contractual. Even art and literature become dreary and dull if transformed into work.

But the idler refuses all work. He will do only that which he finds interesting, pleasurable or amusing. And as soon as his chosen pastime loses its charm, he will immediately cease to follow this course. And so he retains the dilettante's simple delight, avoiding the uninspiring drudgery of professional labour.

☞ ACHIEVEMENT
AMBITION
CAREERISTS

AMBITION

Ambition is an overmastering desire to be vilified by enemies while living and made ridiculous by friends when dead.

AMBROSE BIERCE

✪

Living in a constant chase after gain compels people to expend their spirit to the point of exhaustion in a continual pretence of overreaching and anticipating others.

FRIEDRICH NIETZSCHE

✪

The great-souled man will not compete for the common objects of ambition or go where other people take first place; he will be idle and slow to act.

ARISTOTLE

✪

What a foolish thing it is to be governed by a desire for fame and profit and to fret away one's whole life without a moment of peace.

KENKO YOSHIDA

The Importance of Being Idle

The idler is never ambitious. He does not hanker after self-advancement. He is quite happy to stay exactly where he is. He knows that ambition is the child of dissatisfaction and the father of disenchantment. He realises that even fulfilled ambition produces nothing but unhappiness and despair.

The ambitious man struggles up a hill, pushing his rivals out of his path. The end of his journey is in sight. But when he reaches the top of the hill, he discovers that a loftier mountain exists beyond. The hill he has so laboriously climbed is dwarfed to the point of insignificance by the mountain ahead. And so the journey must continue on to retirement and, perversely, idleness.

☞   ACHIEVEMENT
      CAREERISTS
      SUCCESS
      WORKAHOLICS

ANCIENT GREECE

The Greeks in their era of greatness had only contempt for work. Their slaves alone were permitted to labour: the free man knew only exercises for the body and mind. And so it was in this era that men like Aristotle, Phidias, Aristophanes moved and breathed among the people ... The philosophers of antiquity taught contempt for work, that degradation of the free man, the poets sang of idleness, that gift from the gods.

PAUL LAFARGUE

The great achievements of the Archaic Age of Greek civilisation (from 1200 BC until 500 BC) arose from their leisured society. The ancient Greeks placed great emphasis on the importance of idleness. They believed that indolence was undoubtedly a Good Thing. Aristotle summed up the Greek attitude towards idleness when he used philosophic logic to prove that happiness depends on leisure. In his *Histories*, Herodotus tells us that the Greeks frowned upon manual work. They considered it to be ignoble to sully one's hands with toil.

☞   GREEK PHILOSOPHY
        HERODOTUS

15

ARMCHAIRS

I admit that I do loll about in my friends' drawing rooms ... What are armchairs for, anyway, except for people to loll in?

LIN YUTANG

✪

I love it, I love it; and who shall dare
To chide me for loving that old armchair?

ELIZA COOK

✪

It seems absurd to expect goodness or even good temper from a man who is seated on a hard bench with his body forming a right angle, for joy and geniality are allied to curves rather than to angles ... The armchair is as inimical to fury or peevishness as is a hot bath.

GILBERT QUIN

✪

The inexpressible charms of the elbow-chair, attended with a soft stool for the elevation of the feet! Thus, vacant of thought, do I indulge the live-long day.

SAMUEL JOHNSON

The idler will possess a comfortable armchair and a comfortable bed. If he is not in one, he will be in the other. Ivan Goncharov's Oblomov, the laziest character in Russian literature, spends his days moving from bed to armchair and back again.

    ☞   **BEDS**
                  GETTING OUT OF BED
                  LYING IN BED
                  OBLOMOV
                  SLEEP

BARTELBY THE SCRIVENER

I am a man who, from his youth upward, has been filled with a profound conviction that the easiest way of life is the best.

HERMAN MELVILLE

Herman Melville, the author of *Moby Dick*, wrote a short story about a scrivener named Bartelby, which was published in *Putnam's Monthly* in 1853. A scrivener acted as a human Xerox machine: his task was to copy text – such as legal documents – by hand. For some time, Bartelby was a very diligent scrivener. He did 'an extraordinary quantity of writing. As if long famishing for something to copy, he seemed to gorge himself on documents'. Part of a scrivener's job was to 'verify the accuracy of his copy, word by word ... a dull, wearisome, and lethargic affair'.

Suddenly one day, Bartelby refused to carry out this part of his duties: 'I would prefer not to,' he replied. His boss, the narrator of this tale, was stunned by this refusal and asked again. 'I would prefer not to,' was the reply. Day after day, Bartelby steadfastly refused to examine the documents for accuracy on the grounds that he would prefer not to. His quiet stubbornness was resolute. He was unmoved by all the considerations that might normally stir a person to action.

19

Eventually Bartelby was dismissed from his position. The next day, his boss arrived at the office to find Bartelby already in the office. It seems that he had been there all night. When asked to leave, Bartelby replied – rather predictably – 'I would prefer not to'. For this consummate idler, leaving the building is just too strenuous – regardless of the fact that he has been fired.

Melville's biographer Leon Howard claimed that, 'In the power of his quiet resolution and independence lay one of the mysteries of humanity.' And, one might add, one of the shadowy secrets of everlasting idleness.

☞   EXCUSES
IDLERS
OBLOMOV
RIP VAN WINKLE

BEAU BRUMMELL

I like to have the morning well aired before I get up.

BEAU BRUMMELL

Born in 1778, the son of Lord North's private secretary, George Brummell Esq was the first great dandy and turned being a gentleman of leisure – sharp wit, sartorial elegance and studied languidity – in to an art form. He pioneered the idea of the isolated self as a work of art – no occupation, no visible means of support and definitely no attachments. At Eton and Oxford he was already known for his style rather than his studiousness. An acquaintance of both Byron and Sheridan, he eventually became a protege of the Prince Regent, who finally gave him a commission in the 10th Hussars – a dandified ornamental regiment that accompanied the Prince on his pleasure-seeking travels. Brummell only really got out of bed for the grand social occasions where his exquisitedly mannered quips found their perfect stage. He became a legend for doing nothing but looking divine.

☞   GORING, LORD

BEDS

All one really needs is a divinely attractive bed.

Mrs Winston Guest

☞   ARMCHAIRS
           GETTING OUT OF BED
           LYING IN BED
           SLEEP

BREAKFAST

My altar is the breakfast-tray in the bedroom, laden with the coffee-jug, hot rolls, the morning paper, and the postman's freight of friendly letters.

GILBERT QUIN

An idler's perfect day will start with a good cooked breakfast, but never before lunchtime.

What one chooses to eat is entirely a matter of personal preference. The perfect cooked breakfast would include grilled smoked bacon, fried eggs, succulent oven-cooked sausages, crispy fried bread, and grilled black pudding. This is known, of course, as an English breakfast.

The medical establishment would frown upon such a feast for its high fat content. But fat-rich foods are extremely important. There is firm scientific evidence that fatty foods induce laziness. The presence of certain fatty acids in the digestive system hinders the body's ability to produce energy. A fried breakfast is a useful way of inducing laziness.

☞   AFTERNOON TEA

23

SIR BASIL STANLAKE BROOKE

Sir Basil Stanlake Brooke (1881-1973) was an idle politician – a rare creature indeed. As the *Dictionary of National Biography* records, 'Brooke spent most of his life as a country gentleman … A lazy man of limited ability and considerable charm, he preferred country pursuits, especially fishing, to the work of government.' A colleague recorded that 'those who met him imagined that he was relaxing away from his desk. What they didn't realise was that there was no desk.'

☞ PARLIAMENT

BUCHANITES

The Buchanites were an exceptionally lazy and hedonistic religious sect founded in Irvine in Scotland in 1784. They were named after their founder, Elspeth Buchan. The poet Robert Burns, a contemporary eyewitness, described the cult and their lifestyle:

'They live nearly an idle life, carrying on a great farce of pretended devotion in barns and woods, where they lodge and lie together, and hold likewise a community of women, as it is another of their tenets that they can commit no mortal sin.'

In our own age of demented religious cults, who frequently announce that their God-given mission is to kill themselves or to kill everyone else, a revival of the idle Buchanite cult would be rather welcome. Their ideal was a combination of loafing and free love. Personally I have always had an aversion to suicide and slaughter. I hope I am not alone in saying that, given the choice, I would prefer to devote my life to sloth and sex. So let's all run away to the barns and the woods to become Buchanites.

☞   CHRISTIANITY
      HEAVEN

BUDDHISM

When in doubt whether to do something or to do nothing, it is usually best to do nothing.

> from the Buddhist work known as
> THE ICHIGON HODAN

✪

When you go into retreat at a mountain temple and serve the Buddha, you are never at a loss how to spend your time.

> KENKO YOSHIDA

I don't like to cast aspersions, but have you ever wondered why the Buddha was a big fat chap who spent all his time sitting down? Surely he was an idler. In its desire to reach a state of enlightenment, Buddhism's major tools are meditation and contemplation — activities regarded by cynics as nothing more than religious loafing. The *Maka Shikan*, a basic text of Tendai Buddhism, advises you to 'Break your ties with your daily activities, with personal affairs, with your arts, and with learning.'

☞ KENKO YOSHIDA
   MONASTICISM

26

BUSINESS

Business with its continuous work has become a necessary part of our lives ... a man exists for the sake of his business, instead of the reverse.

MAX WEBER

✪

The really idle man gets nowhere. The perpetually busy man does not get much further.

SIR HENEAGE OGLIVIE

✪

Business, it seems to me, consists of pitting brain and hand and artifice against one's neighbour for the acquisition of money and power, and that in turn resolves itself into riding to fortune upon the backs of the less fortunate. Perhaps that is why ill-fortune and idleness are associated – as an excuse for the wealthy.

GILBERT QUIN

✪

Business was his aversion; pleasure was his business.

MARIA EDGEWORTH

The Importance of Being Idle

The shining example of finest-quality, steam-rolled,
double-twilled men of business, amidst whom my
youth was spent, never once led me astray, nor
induced me to dissipate in an orgy of money-making
that energy for Idling which was Nature's choicest
gift.

WALTER RAYMOND

✪

'It is the fashion nowadays,' said Clovis, 'to talk about
the romance of Business. There isn't such a thing.
The romance has all been the other way, with the idle
apprentice, the truant, the runaway, the individual
who couldn't be bothered with figures and book-
keeping and left business to look after itself ...
On the other side of the account there is the
industrious apprentice, who grew up into the business
man, married early and worked late, and lived,
thousands and thousands of him, in little villas
outside big towns. He is buried by the thousand in
Kensal Green and other large cemeteries; any romance
that was ever in him was buried prematurely in shop
and warehouse and office. Whenever I feel in the
least tempted to be business-like or methodical or
even decently industrious I go to Kensal Green and
look at the graves of those who died in business.'

SAKI

More evil is done under the cloak of business than was ever contemplated by all the idlers the earth has known.

GILBERT QUIN

☞ INDUSTRY

29

BUSY BEES

Sitting for hours idle in the shade of an apple tree, near the garden-hives, and under the aerial thoroughfares of those honey-merchants ... I have sought instruction from the Bees, and tried to appropriate to myself the old industrious lesson. And yet, hang it all, who by rights should be the teacher and who the learners? For those peevish, over-toiled, utilitarian insects, was there no lesson to be derived from the spectacle of Me? Gazing out at me with myriad eyes from their joyless factories, might they not learn at last – could I not finally teach them – a wiser and more generous-hearted way to improve the shining hours?

LOGAN PEARSALL SMITH

How doth the little fussy bee
Waste all the shining hours,
In working hard for you and me
Amongst the idle flowers!

She gathers honey all the while
Throughout the summer day:
The Idler passes with a smile
And takes it all away!

The daily round I'll gladly shirk,
I would be idle too;
Thank goodness there is still some work
An Idler does not do.

In books, or ease, or healthful play,
Let all my life be passed,
That I may have, for any day,
No vain regrets at last.

A Few Odd Reflections on Idleness
VYVYAN HOLLAND

AFTER DINNER ONE EVENING, A FRIEND OF mine began espousing the benefits of business. When I challenged him on this, he tried to silence me with an epigram.

'One should devote one days to the sins of business and one's nights to the business of sins,' he declared, hoping that the reference to sins would be sufficiently hedonistic for my tastes.

'Business — a laborious nothing that leads to lassitude,' I replied, pausing to take a sip of port. 'I'm quoting Byron, but I don't expect you to recognise it. Very few people seem to read Byron these days.'

'I would like to read more,' my friend objected, 'but I don't have enough spare time.'

'Not enough spare time,' I repeated, looking as smug as one can with a painfully full stomach. 'And with that,' I continued, 'I rest my case. The benefits of business have been exposed. "Let us talk in tender horrors of our loathing all kinds of toil." And yes, before you ask, that's Byron again.'

BUSY IDLENESS

I love idleness. I love to busy myself about trifles, to begin a hundred things and not finish one of them, to come and go as my fancy bids me, to change my mind every moment, to follow a fly in all its circlings, to try to uproot a rock to see what is underneath, eagerly to begin on a ten-years' task and to give up after ten minutes: in short, to fritter away the whole day inconsequentially and incoherently, and to follow nothing but the whim of the moment.

JEAN JACQUES ROUSSEAU

✪

There is no kind of idleness, by which we are so easily seduced, as that which dignifies itself by the appearance of business, and by making the loiterer imagine that he has something to do which must not be neglected, keeps him in perpetual agitation, and hurries him rapidly from place to place.

SAMUEL JOHNSON

Somebody has said that dust is matter in the wrong place. The same definition applies to nine-tenths of those called lazy. They are people gone astray in a direction that does not answer to their temperament nor to their capacities. In reading the biography of great men, we are struck with the number of 'idlers' among them. They were lazy so long as they had not found the right path; afterwards they became laborious to excess. Darwin, Stephenson, and may others belong to this category of idlers.

PETER KROPOTKIN

I am no mere thinker, no mere creature of dreams and imagination. I pay bills, post letters; I buy new bootlaces and put them in my boots. And when I set out to get my hair cut, it is with the iron face of those men of empire and unconquerable will, those Caesars and Napoleons, whose footsteps shake the earth.

LOGAN PEARSALL SMITH

☞   IDLENESS
        INDOLENCE
        LOAFING

CAREERISTS

The trouble with the rat race is that even if you win, you're still a rat.

LILY TOMLIN

★

He is blind, and deaf, and dumb to everything in the world but his office. But he will get on, he will be somebody to be reckoned with one day, hold a high rank in the service ... It's called making a career! But it's wasting a man: intelligence, will, feeling are not wanted; a mere luxury! He will go through life and a great deal in him will never be awakened.

IVAN GONCHAROV

There is a sort of dead-alive hackneyed people about, who are scarcely conscious of living except in the exercise of some conventional occupation ... It is no good speaking to such folk: they cannot be idle, their nature is not generous enough ... When they do not require to go to the office, when they are not hungry and have no mind to drink, the whole breathing world is a blank to them.

ROBERT LOUIS STEVENSON

☞ AMBITION
AMATEURS
WORKAHOLICS

THOMAS CHALMERS

Thomas Chalmers (1780-1847) was a lazy theologian who occasionally made the effort to preach. In a famous incident, his sermonising caused the Prime Minister to burst into tears. Several members of his Cabinet immediately emulated this lachrymosity. Historians have never been able to agree on the significance of this episode. Anyway, Chalmers, according to his friend Thomas Carlyle, was 'a man capable of much soaking indolence, lazy brooding and do-nothingism.'

CHRISTIANITY

People may say what they like about the decay of Christianity; the religious system that produced green Chartreuse can never really die.

S<small>AKI</small>

✪

Go back ... to the very beginning. What was Adam, I should like to know, but a loafer? Did he do anything but loaf? Who is foolish enough to say that Adam was a working man? Who dare aver that he dealt in stocks, or was busy in the sugar line?

W<small>ALT</small> W<small>HITMAN</small>

Christianity should have nothing against idleness. Jesus in his Sermon on the Mount preached idleness: 'Consider the lilies of the field, how they grow: they toil not, neither do they spin' (Matthew 6:28-29). Jesus may well have been following the example set by his dad, God. After six days of work, the Creator decided that he would not create anymore; instead he would rest for all eternity. Nietzsche claimed that God is dead. This is incorrect. God's not dead. He's just loafing.

☞   HEAVEN
        MONASTICISM
        PROTESTANT WOTK ETHIC
        SEVEN DEADLY SINS

CIVILISATION

Civilisation is, in its earliest days, played. It does not come from play like a babe detaching itself from the womb: it arises in and as play, and never leaves it.

JOHANN HUIZINGA

✪

How did the human scamp begin his ascent to civilisation? What were the first signs of promise in him, or of his developing intelligence? The answer is undoubtedly to be found in man's playful curiosity, in his first efforts to fumble about with his hands and turn everything inside out to examine it, as a monkey in his idle moments turns the eyelid or ear-lobe of a fellow-monkey, looking for lice or for nothing at all – just turning about for turning about's sake. Go to the zoo and watch a pair of monkeys picking each other's ears, and there you have the promise of an Isaac Newton or an Albert Einstein.

LIN YUTANG

The Importance of Being Idle

Leisure has a value of its own. It is not a mere hand-maid of labour; it is something we should know how to cultivate, to use, and to enjoy. It has a distinct and honourable place wherever nations are released from the pressure of their first rude needs, their first homely toil, and rise to happier levels of grace and intellectual repose.

AGNES REPPLIER

✪

Civilisation, in its first outcome, is heavily in the debt of leisure; and the success of any society worth considering is to be estimated largely by the use to which its fortunati put their spare moments.

HENRY BLAKE FULLER

✪

The leisure class ... contributed nearly the whole of what we call civilisation. It cultivated the arts and discovered the sciences; it wrote the books, invented the philosophies, and refined social relations ... Without the leisure class, mankind would never have emerged from barbarism.

BERTRAND RUSSELL

Increased means and increased leisure are the two civilisers of man.

BENJAMIN DISRAELI

✪

Culture is essentially a product of leisure. The art of culture is therefore essentially the art of loafing.

LIN YUTANG

✪

Is the ant so much more to be envied than the grasshopper, because she spends her life in grubbing and storing, and can spend no time for singing?

JEROME K JEROME

What, you might ask, is 'civilisation'? A dictionary will tell you that civilisation is the opposite of that primitive state of being in which homo sapiens developed. Not an especially helpful definition, you must admit, but a useful point at which to start. We must examine this 'primitive state of being' and envisage its opposite before we can understand the meaning of 'civilisation'.

The primitive state of being was not very nice. The prehistoric human spent all his waking hours grubbing around in the dirt for his food, foraging in the woods for berries. All in all, it was fairly hard work. And, at the end

41

of this exhausting day, the poor creature was so worn out that a decent night's rest would have been welcome. But this was never achieved. After nightfall, the larger predators came looking for him, to remind him of place in the animal kingdom. He was lucky if he could snatch forty winks up a tree with one eye open. Clearly this was not a satisfactory way of life. Always hungry, always alert, always working hard to survive, and never at peace – this was the primitive state of being.

As we have already established, civilisation is the opposite of this. In a civilised community, therefore, people should have plenty of food, continuous tranquillity, and a great deal of rest. The civilised man should have a full stomach after every meal, a good night's sleep at the end of the day, and nothing especially arduous to do. The conclusion is unavoidable: 'civilisation' should represent a luxurious combination of good food and idleness. So why should we still have to waste all our waking hours grubbing? Something surely is amiss?

☞   FORD, HENRY
        LEISURE
        PLAY

CLOTHES

The dressing gown had a number of invaluable qualities in Oblomov's eyes: it was soft and pliable; it did not get in his way; it obeyed the least movement of his body, like a docile slave. Oblomov never wore a tie or a waistcoat at home because he liked comfort and freedom. He wore long, soft, wide slippers; when he got up from bed he put his feet straight into them without looking.

IVAN GONCHAROV

✪

The stroke of eleven in the morning is still as terrible to me as before, and I find putting on my clothes still as painful and laborious. Oh that our climate would permit that original nakedness which the thrice happy Indians to this day enjoy! How many unsolicitous hours should I bask away, warmed in bed by the sun's glorious beams, could I, like them, tumble from thence in a moment, when necessity obliges me to endure the torment of getting upon my legs.

SAMUEL JOHNSON

The Importance of Being Idle

Why each morning do we get up and wash and dress ourselves, to undress ourselves at night and go to bed again?

JEROME K JEROME

 OBLOMOV

SAMUEL TAYLOR COLERIDGE

I am a dreaming and therefore an indolent man.

SAMUEL TAYLOR COLERIDGE

Samuel Taylor Coleridge (1772-1834) is remembered primarily as a poet of rare ability, famous in particular for The Rime of the Ancient Mariner and Kubla Khan, but he was celebrated during his lifetime as an eminent philosopher. As a true idler, detached from the strenuous reality of life, he observed the unproductive turbulence of the foolish world.

In 1798 and 1799 he contributed on an occasional basis to the Morning Post. In 1800 he was offered £2,000 a year – an enormous sum in those days – to work for this newspaper full-time, a choice which would have meant abandoning the rustic tranquillity of Keswick in the Lake District for the ceaseless hullabaloo of London. His response made clear his belief that idleness is too precious to be exchanged for cash: 'I would not give up the country and the lazy reading of old folios for two thousand times £2,000 a year.'

☞ POETRY

CONTEMPLATION

Contemplation is but a glorious title to idleness.

SIR PHILIP SIDNEY

☞   CREATIVITY
IMAGINATION
INTELLECTUALS

CONTEMPLATION, I SAID, 'IS OFTEN THE idler's sole activity.'
'Activity,' my friend replied, 'is a dangerously energetic word.'
'Indeed,' I said, 'but contemplation requires no effort beyond the ordinary and unavoidable working of the brain. From contemplation, great things flow.' I paused in contemplation, hoping to prove my point with some timeless and epigrammatic observation on the condition of humanity, but to no avail. We sat in silence, and I lit a cigarette.

CREATIVITY

If the mind wandering free be accounted idle, then indeed were Keats and Chopin, Reynolds and R L Stevenson mere idle fellows, for poetry and artistry and song know no office hours.

GILBERT QUIN

☞   ACHIEVEMENT
      IMAGINATION
      LITERATURE
      THOMAS MORE,
      POETRY

47

CRIME

The lazy man is preserved from the commission of almost all the nastier crimes.

EVELYN WAUGH

★

One thing must be said for idleness: it keeps people from doing the Devil's work. The great villains of history were busy men, since great crimes and slaughters require great industry and dedication.

PHILIP SLATER

CURIOSITY

The art is to fill the day with petty business, to have
always something in hand which may raise curiosity,
but not solicitude, and keep the mind in a state of
action, but not of labour.

SAMUEL JOHNSON

✪

Disinterested intellectual curiosity is the lifeblood of
real civilisation.

G M TREVELYAN

✪

Curiosity is one of the permanent and certain
characteristics of a vigorous intellect ... The idler is
always inquisitive.

SAMUEL JOHNSON

☞ CIVILISATION
INTELLECTUALS

DEATH

He slept beneath the moon,
He basked beneath the sun;
He lived a life of going-to-do,
And died with nothing done.

The epitaph of Jas. Albery

☞   DOING NOTHING
         HEAVEN
         LIFE

CHARLES DICKENS

Mr Thomas Idle and Mr Francis Goodchild …
were both idle in the last degree. Between Francis
and Thomas, however, there was this difference of
character: Goodchild was laboriously idle, and would
take upon himself any amount of pains and labour
to assure himself that he was idle; in short, had no
better idea of idleness than that it was useless
industry. Thomas Idle, on the other hand, was an
idler of the unmixed Irish or Neapolitan type; a
passive idler, a born-and-bred idler, a consistent idler,
who practised what he would have preached if he had
not been too idle to preach; a one entire and perfect
chrysolite of idleness.

CHARLES DICKENS

The extract above is taken from *The Lazy Tour of Two Idle
Apprentices*, one of Dickens' lesser known works. It was
published in instalments, like much of his writing, in the
pages of *Household Works*. The story of these 'apprentices
to Literature' is a thinly disguised account of Dickens'
tour of the north of England in 1857 in the company of
his friend Wilkie Collins. Francis Goodchild represents
Charles Dickens, and Thomas Idle is Wilkie Collins.
Dickens was never an idler: he was 'laboriously idle' like
so many workaholics who chastise themselves for laziness
after a great deal of hard work. Collins, on the other

hand, was — at least according to Dickens — an authentic idler who saw loafing as the true purpose of life.

☞   **LITERATURE**

DOING NOTHING

When things are going to rack and ruin, the most purposeful act may be to sit still.

Henry Miller

✪

The most precious, the most consoling, the most pure and holy, the noble habit of doing nothing at all.

G K Chesterton

✪

Every now and then, be completely idle – do nothing at all.

Sydney Smith

My most intense pleasure is to walk or sit doing nothing. My favourite occupation is picking useless stuff (leaves, straw, and so on) and doing useless things.

ANTON CHEKHOV

✪

Do not put off until tomorrow what can be put off till the day-after-tomorrow just as well.

MARK TWAIN

✪

Idleness is not doing nothing. Idleness is being free to do anything.

FLOYD DELL

✪

How beautiful it is to do nothing, and then rest afterwards.

SPANISH PROVERB

✪

The perfect man does nothing. The sage takes no action.

CHUANG-TSE

I do nothing, granted. But I see the hours pass –
which is better than trying to fill them.

E M Cioran

✪

I always feel an inclination to do nothing.

Samuel Johnson

✪

Positively the best thing a man can have to do is
nothing, and, next to that, perhaps, good works.

Charles Lamb

✪

It is awfully hard work doing nothing.

Oscar Wilde

✪

He that sits still, or reposes himself upon a couch, no
more deceives himself than he deceives others; he
knows that he is doing nothing.

Samuel Johnson

☞   IDLENESS
LAZINESS

JOSEPH VON EICHENDORFF

I felt as if I would collapse from sheer indolence.

JOSEPH VON EICHENDORFF

Baron Joseph von Eichendorff (1788-1857) was a German author at the forefront of nineteenth-century Romantic Movement. His best-known work is a romance entitled *Aus dem Leben eines Taugenichts*. This translates into English as *The Memoirs of a Good-for-Nothing*, although one translator rendered it as *The Love Frolics of a Young Scamp*, which conveys the idea of the book rather more accurately.

The adventure began with this young man's father berating him for his idleness. 'You good-for-nothing,' complained the old man. 'There you are sunning yourself again, stretching your bones till they ache.' Our young scamp was not unduly concerned, and replied that he would go 'out into the world' to make his fortune.

So he ran off to Vienna and got a job as a gardener's assistant. He liked the gardens ('I liked the temples and groves and attractive avenues, and would have gladly strolled along them at my leisure') but disliked the job ('there was unfortunately a good deal of work to do'). He moved on, therefore, and got a job as a toll keeper: 'since I had no real duties to perform, I sat all day on the little seat in front of the house, wearing a dressing-gown and a night-cap, and smoking a long pipe'.

'Italy is a beautiful country where God Himself provides for all,' said a passer-by one day. 'You can lie on your back in the sun and the grapes will drop into your mouth.' Our good-for-nothing needed no more encouragement: he left for Italy in the company of two young painters who told him that if he stayed with them he could be on holiday all the time.

In the middle of the night, however, the painters departed unexpectedly, so our young scamp continued the journey to Italy on his own. Fortunately he was able to travel in a comfortable coach: 'I stretched myself out in the coach,' he tells us, 'as though I were lying on a sofa.' But the coachman, who was rather maniacal, took him against his will to a mysterious castle in which he was made to stay. 'I enjoyed it to the full,' our narrator tells us. 'I slept in a grand four-poster bed, and went for strolls in the garden, played on my violin … I would lie for hours in the long grass.'

Having escaped from this castle after the inhabitants tried to kill him, he wandered around the countryside searching for his 'lovely lady' – a girl with whom he had fallen in love. Eventually he found her. Unsurprisingly, they lived happily ever after. As you may have gathered, idleness permeates the entire tale. *Aus dem Leben eines Taugenichts* indeed.

☞   LITERATURE

EMPLOYMENT

Nature has made neither shoemaker nor smith. Such occupations degrade the people who exercise them.

PLATO

✪

The citizens must not live the life of mechanics or shopkeepers, which is ignoble and inimical to goodness. Nor can those who are to be citizens engage in farming; leisure is a necessity, both for growth in goodness and for the pursuit of political activities.

ARISTOTLE

✪

A gentleman ... sleeps at his work. That's what work's for. Why do you think they have the SILENCE notices in the library? So as not to disturb me in my little nook behind the biography shelves.

ALAN AYCKBOURN

✪

George goes to sleep at a bank from ten to four each day, except Saturdays, when they wake him up and put him outside at two.

JEROME K JEROME

There are wealthy gentlemen in England who drive
four-horse passenger-coaches twenty or thirty miles
on a daily line, in the summer, because the privilege
costs them considerable money; but if they were
offered wages for the service that would turn it into
work, then they would resign.

MARK TWAIN

✪

When a niece of his joyfully told him how her
husband had at last found a job, Uncle Bertie replied,
'Oh, my dear, I'm so sorry'.

NELSON W ALDRICH

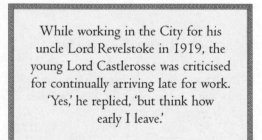

While working in the City for his
uncle Lord Revelstoke in 1919, the
young Lord Castlerosse was criticised
for continually arriving late for work.
'Yes,' he replied, 'but think how
early I leave.'

☞   **CAREERISTS**
WORK
WORKAHOLICS

ENDYMION

Endymion sleeps forever, remaining deathless and ageless.

APOLLODORUS

In Greek mythology, Endymion was an indolent young shepherd of exceptional beauty. As he lay sleeping on Mount Latmos, the moon goddess Selene was enchanted by his graceful appearance and instantly fell in love with him. When the Olympian gods discovered her secret, Zeus offered Endymion perpetual youth on the condition that he remain asleep forever. Eternally young, forever beautiful, and adored by the foolish moon above, Endymion sleeps on.

☞ ANCIENT GREECE
    SOMNUS
    SEVEN SLEEPERS OF
        EPHESUS

ENERGY

Very often the idler is but a man to whom it is
repugnant to spend all his life making the eighteenth
part of a pin, or the hundredth part of a watch,
while he feels he has exuberant energy which he
would like to expend elsewhere.

PETER KROPOTKIN

✪

I am happiest when I am idle. I could live for months
without performing any kind of labour, and at the
expiration of that time I should feel fresh and
vigorous enough to go right on in the same way for
numerous more months.

ARTEMUS WARD

It is a common fallacy that the idler lacks energy.
The roots of this misunderstanding are not hard to
discover. The idler certainly does appear to be lethargic:
he lounges languidly, looking very much like a man
deficient of dynamism. Sometimes, indeed, one might
even suspect that his condition borders on chronic
narcolepsy. But this appearance is deceptive. A lack of
energy is neither the cause nor the product of his
idleness.

Only hard work and exertion can produce a debilitat-
ing lack of energy. Idleness, on the other hand, is an

energising force. It refreshes the idler and gives him strength. Of course, he always chooses to save this energy rather than squander it on pointless activity, and for this he must be commended.

☞   **IDLENESS
WEARINESS**

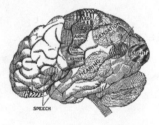

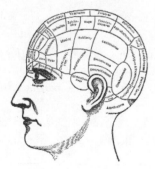

EVOLUTION: THE DEVELOPMENT OF THE HUMAN BRAIN

Human history can be thought to have begun with the development of rational thought. This ability to reason logically was what first set us apart from the rest of the animal kingdom. Here the usual evolutionary explanation of survival of the fittest will not suffice. The idea of survival of the fittest applies only to physical characteristics – the ways in which animals became efficient machines. The ancestor of the giraffe, for example, prospered when he was able to eat leaves from the tops of tall trees. So those primitive giraffes with longer necks survived to mate and the 'long-neck' gene eventually became deeply embedded in the DNA of that animal. The giraffe's long neck is essentially an efficient machine for eating the leaves at the top of trees.

But the development of the human brain was not at all similar. The human brain is not a simple machine like a limb or an extra-long neck. The development of rational thought was not essential for survival – we are the only animals that have it, and all the other animals survive without it. Whereas normal evolution is the product of adaptation as a result of struggle and hardship, the development of the brain was the product of different circumstances. It is to these circumstances that we must turn.

The Importance of Being Idle

It has been discovered that the first steps in the path towards rational thought were taken in a fertile area of the Sahara basin. This area was highly unusual, because here food was abundant and predators were scarce. Primitive humans did not need to forage for food all day and fend off fiends all night. Here primitive humans had plenty of spare time for leisure and relaxation.

Early man started to think in a rational manner because he sat around all day. In the fertile Sahara basin there was no need to work hard to survive, so primitive man could idle his time away by attempting to work out solutions to everyday problems by playing with ideas. The development of rational thought was the consequence — a rather useful product of idleness, don't you think?

☞ MANKIND

EXCUSES

There is always tomorrow.

RUSSIAN PROVERB

The idler usually fails to do as he is asked, especially when the allotted task requires any great effort on his part. So very often the idler will need to give an excuse. He will be called upon to explain his lack of action. The authentic idler cannot say 'I was too busy'. No one would believe this excuse for a moment.

So he has to use other excuses. 'I'll do it tomorrow,' he says, safe in the knowledge that tomorrow never comes. 'Mañana, mañana,' says the Spanish idler. But this disingenuous excuse can wear thin, so more excuses will be needed. The idler could claim that he had been unwell, but he is well known as a hypochondriac already. He could, perhaps, claim that he did not know how to complete the required task, but pride prevents most idlers from making such an admission. Of course, the best excuse is always the truth: 'I would prefer not to'.

☞   **BARTELBY THE SCRIVENER
HYPOCHONDRIA**

HENRY FORD

There is no place in civilisation for the idler. None of us has any right to ease.

HENRY FORD

Henry Ford, the founder of the Ford automobile empire, was a narrow-minded industrialist, a man whose sole aim in life was to increase the productivity of his factories. He is remembered fondly by capitalists everywhere as the man responsible for the introduction of assembly-line techniques in factories and the subsequent boom in productivity levels throughout America.

The workers, of course, were not fond of this innovative practice. The unpleasant monotony of this assembly-line work led to the resignation of half of Ford's workforce in 1914, and he was forced to offer double the wage paid by other industrialists before people became willing to endure the mind-numbing boredom of the conveyer belt.

☞   CIVILISATION
RIGHTS

FREEDOM

What is liberty? Leisure. What is leisure? Liberty.

GEORGE BERNARD SHAW

✪

Work makes a mockery of freedom ...
a worker is a part-time slave.

BOB BLACK

☞   CREATIVITY
              RIGHTS
              SLAVERY

GETTING OUT OF BED

It was such a lovely day. I thought it was a pity to get up.

WILLIAM SOMERSET MAUGHAM

✪

Ah! How delicious it is to turn over and go to sleep again 'just for five minutes.' Is there any human being, I wonder, besides the hero of a Sunday-school 'tale for boys,' who ever gets up willingly? There are some men to whom getting up at the proper time is an utter impossibility.

JEROME K JEROME

✪

There are some that profess idleness in its full dignity … who boast that they do nothing, and thank their stars that they have nothing to do; who sleep every night till they can sleep no longer, and rise only that exercise may enable them to sleep again; who prolong the reign of darkness by double curtains, and never see the sun but to 'tell him how they hate his beams', whose whole labour is to vary the postures of indulgence, and whose day differs from their night but as a couch or chair differs from a bed.

SAMUEL JOHNSON

The Importance of Being Idle

I am content to base my belief in the virtues of
leisurely arising upon the knowledge that I am not of
that company of giants who awake clear-eyed in the
keen air and dim half-light of the winter's morn, hurl
the blankets from their recumbent forms, and plunge
with gay abandon into the enticing embrace of a cold
bath. My gods and not their gods; I worship at a
different shrine.

GILBERT QUIN

✪

Dawn is the time when men of reason go to bed.
Certain old men prefer to rise at about that time,
taking a cold bath and a long walk with an empty
stomach, and otherwise mortifying the flesh ...
The reason we find only robust persons doing this
thing is that it has killed all the others who have
tried it.

AMBROSE BIERCE

✪

Rise early. It is the early bird that catches the worm.
Don't be fooled by this absurd law; I once knew a
man who tried it. He got up at sunrise and a horse
bit him. Wisdom teaches us that none but birds
should go out early, and that not even birds should
do it unless they are out of worms.

MARK TWAIN

Early to rise and early to bed, makes a male healthy
and wealthy and dead.

JAMES THURBER

In Frisby-on-the-Wreake (a small village in Leicester-
shire) is a building called Zion House, which, after its
construction in 1725, became an 'Academy for Young
Gentlemen'. It is said that the schoolmaster and his
pupils were not early risers. One morning a couplet was
seen chalked on the shutters of the window: Cheer up
my friends – pray do not weep,/We are not dead but
fast asleep.

☞   **BEDS**
        LYING IN BED

GREEK PHILOSOPHY

All the old philosophers were loafers. Take Diogenes
for instance. He lived in a tub, and demeaned himself
like a true child of the great loafer family.

WALT WHITMAN

The ancient Greeks were the first to seek wisdom for its
own sake. The word 'philosophy' is a combination of two
words: philos, meaning love; and sophia, meaning
wisdom. The verb philosopheo means 'to love wisdom'.
Philosophy – the pursuit of wisdom for its own sake –
is the root of all academic disciplines.

Philosophy developed as a result of idling. The
Greeks believed idleness led to discussion, and discussion
led to wisdom. Many of the key works of Greek philosophy are written as dialogues as this is how their ideas
were arrived at – in idle conversation. It is interesting to
look at the development of the Greek word schole,
which originally meant 'leisure' or 'rest'. Gradually it
came to mean 'learned discussion' or 'philosophical
debate'. Eventually, the word schole evolved to become
'school' in modern English. Our words 'school' and
'scholar' come from the ancient Greek word for 'leisure'
or 'rest'.

*　*　*

The birth of Greek philosophy took place during the first half of the first millennium BC in Miletus, an island in the south of Ionia. Miletus was a tremendous place because the Milesians were an uncommonly prosperous lot. In Miletus, food was plentiful, and the Milesians ate well. They did not have to scamper around incessantly to find the next meal. After a good dinner, they were able to sit around and think.

One Milesian in particular, a man named Thales, born in 625 BC is credited as the founder of Greek and therefore European philosophy. Sitting around idling all day, he stumbled upon some rather useful things. He was the first to realise that a circle is bisected by its diameter. He was the first to recognise that the angles at the base of an isosceles triangle are equal. He discovered that when two straight lines intersect each other, the opposite angles are equal. One day he discovered that a right-angled triangle would fit inside a circle, and he was so happy that he sacrificed an ox in celebration. A feast ensued, no doubt. In addition, he produced many geometrical theorems for sailors to use when judging distances. He charted the stars so that men could navigate their boats by night. He was able to predict solar eclipses with great accuracy. He discovered that a year is three hundred and sixty-five days long. He died in 545 BC, aged eighty, in an age when the average life expectancy of a man was twenty-seven. It is undeniable that a life of gentle idleness will be a long and happy one. Thales died as he lived – idling. He was lazing in the hot sun, watching a gymnastic contest, when he fell asleep, never to wake up.

☞   ANCIENT GREECE
HERODOTUS
PHLOSOPHY

LORD GORING

MABEL CHILTERN: Why do you call Lord Goring good-for-nothing?
LORD CAVERSHAM: Because he leads such an idle life.
MABEL CHILTERN: How can you say such a thing? Why, he rides in the Row at ten o'clock in the morning, goes to the Opera three times a week, changes his clothes at least five times a day, and dines out every night of the season. You don't call that leading an idle life, do you?

'Allow me to introduce you to Lord Goring, the idlest man in London,' announces Sir Robert Chiltern, and with this we meet the leading character in Oscar Wilde's play *An Ideal Husband*. Goring is the epitome of the idle dandy. He dresses in the height of fashion and spends his time lounging in armchairs. His life is spent flitting from the fashionable salons to the fashionable clubs and back again. 'I love talking about nothing. It's the only thing I know anything about,' he says, languidly. Lord Goring has a strong hedonistic streak. When his father Lord Caversham accuses him of living entirely for pleasure, the response is typically blasé: 'What else is there to live for, father?' he asks.

☞   OSCAR WILDE

HAPPINESS

There is no complete happiness without complete idleness.

ANTON CHEKHOV

✪

If a person cannot be happy without remaining idle, idle he should remain.

ROBERT LOUIS STEVENSON

✪

To the idler all days are festivals.

TURKISH PROVERB

✪

Happiness is a contemplative activity ... happiness depends on leisure.

ARISTOTLE

☞   MONEY

'Happiness,' I said, 'depends on leisure.'

'It most certainly does not,' my companion interjected.

'Are you questioning the wisdom of Aristotle?' I asked.

'Happiness,' he continued, ignoring my query, 'depends on money. With sufficient capital at his disposal, any man can be happy.'

'I know many miserable millionaires who will doubt your wisdom,' I announced, 'and I am aware of a small but significant number of happy paupers who will confirm the veracity of Aristotle's observation.'

'Anyone who says that money can't buy happiness simply doesn't know where to shop,' my companion declaimed.

'And some of our most wealthy men are often too busy to go shopping,' I added. 'A little spare time would not go amiss.'

HARD WORK

It's true hard work never killed anybody, but I figure why take the chance?

RONALD REAGAN

✪

Few men ever drop dead from overwork, but many curl up and die because of undersatisfaction.

SYDNEY J HARRIS

☞   WORK
      WORKAHOLICS

HEALTH

Descanzar es salud – rest is healthful.

SPANISH PROVERB

The idler has had time to take care of his health and his spirits; he has been a great deal in the open air, which is the most salutary of all things for both body and mind.

ROBERT LOUIS STEVENSON

☞ STRESS

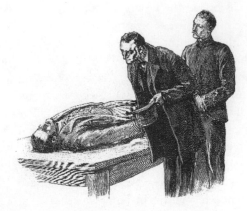

HEAVEN

Great is the idleness that prevails in Heaven.
                                                    JUVENAL

Juvenal's remark is entirely sensible. I refuse to consider, even for one moment, the ridiculous suggestion that such a cruel thing as Work could possibly exist in Heaven. Work is a profane, worldly phenomenon; it is not spiritual or celestial. With no work at all in Heaven, the idleness prevailing therein must indeed be great and all encompassing. A group of angels sunbathe, stretched out on comfortable clouds, whilst others loll in the shade, plucking nonchalantly on ornate golden harps. Seated in his comfy chair, God snoozes peacefully after a large lunch. This splendid existence is the just reward for those who discovered the beauty of complete idleness in the course of their lives on earth.

If Hell is the antithesis of Heaven, it must be accepted that there is no idleness in Hell. The Devil and his minions stand, like slave drivers, presiding over an exhausted population of souls who are forced to work for all eternity. Great is the toil that prevails in Hell, as Juvenal might have said. This is the punishment for those who rejected idleness on earth and committed the sin of wasting their time on the fruitless pursuit of earthly gain. This is the castigation for those who noticed only the transient achievements of human exertion.

☞   CHRISTIANITY
           MONASTICISM
           PROTESTANT WORK ETHIC
           SEVEN DEADLY SINS

HERODOTUS

In Book Two of his *Histories*, written in the second half of the fifth century BC, Herodotus tells us of Amasis, a king of Egypt, who was notoriously idle. One day a group of men came to see Amasis to complain about his idleness. Herodotus' report of the response given by Amasis deserves to be quoted in full:

'Archers,' Amasis replied, 'string their bows when they wish to shoot, and unstring them after use. A bow kept always strung would break, and so be useless when it was needed. It is the same with a man: anyone who was always serious, and never allowed himself a fair share of relaxation and amusement, would suddenly go mad or die of a stroke. It is because I know this that I divide my time between duty and pleasure.'

It is safe to assume that Herodotus's audience would have approved of the sentiment expressed by Amasis — their antipathy to work and their desire to avoid being highly strung was a strong as his.

☞   ANCIENT GREECE

HISTORY

These curiosities would be quite forgot, did not such idle fellows as I am put them down.

JOHN AUBREY

✪

The pleasantest of all diversions is to sit alone under the lamp, a book spread out before you, and to make friends with people of a distant past you have never known.

KENKO YOSHIDA

HOLIDAYS

I wish that all the year were holiday.

CHARLES LAMB

✪

We should seek out some retired old-world spot, far from the madding crowd, and dream away a sunny week among its drowsy lanes – some half-forgotten nook, hidden away by the fairies, out of reach of the noisy world – some quaint-perched eyrie on the cliffs of Time.

JEROME K JEROME

HOUSEWORK

Woman's work! Housework's the hardest work in the world. That's why men won't do it.

EDNA FERBER

HYPOCHONDRIA

What it was that was actually the matter with us, we none of us could be sure of; but the unanimous opinion was that it – whatever it was – had been brought on by overwork.

'What we want is rest,' said Harris.

'Rest and a complete change,' said George. 'The overstrain upon our brains has produced a general depression throughout the system. Change of scene, and absence of the necessity for thought, will restore the mental equilibrium.'

JEROME K JEROME

☞　　EXCUSES

IDENTITY

A faculty for idleness implies … a strong sense of personal identity.

ROBERT LOUIS STEVENSON

★

It is in his pleasures that a man really lives, it is from his leisure that he constructs the true fabric of self.

AGNES REPPLIER

IDLENESS

The blessing of idleness came to me as a birthright, and never, except under coercion, spending a moment in unprofitable work, I have held to it in spite of all the world's temptations.

WALTER RAYMOND

✪

Of all our passions the one we are least cognisant of is idleness.

LA ROCHEFOUCAULD

✪

We might make ourselves spiritual by detaching ourselves from action, and become perfect by the rejection of energy.

OSCAR WILDE

✪

As peace is the end of war, so to be idle is the ultimate purpose of the busy.

SAMUEL JOHNSON

✪

Better to idle well than to work badly.

SPANISH PROVERB

Work is not always required ... there is such a thing as sacred idleness, the cultivation of which is now fearfully neglected.

GEORGE MACDONALD

✪

The sweetness of being idle.

TACITUS

✪

Idleness predominates in many lives where it is not suspected, for being a vice which terminates in itself, it may be enjoyed without injury to others, and is therefore not watched like fraud, which endangers property, or like pride which naturally seeks its gratifications in another's inferiority. Idleness is a silent and peaceful quality, that neither raises envy by ostentation, nor hatred by opposition; and therefore nobody is busy to censure or detect it.

SAMUEL JOHNSON

✪

Idleness so-called, which does not consist in doing nothing, but in doing a great deal not recognised in the dogmatic formularies of the ruling class, has as good a right to state its position as industry itself.

ROBERT LOUIS STEVENSON

The Importance of Being Idle

Time was when we grudged other folk their measure
Of Idleness – Oh! most exalted niche,
Wherein the hours are spent pursuing pleasure.

ROBERT ATKINSON

✪

Masterly inactivity.

HORACE

✪

The fatigue even of thinking becomes more painful
to me every day. I love to dream, but freely, letting
my mind wander about without enslaving myself to
any subject … This idle and contemplative life, which
you do not approve, and I make no excuses for,
becomes to me more delicious daily. To wander alone
endlessly and ceaselessly among the trees and rocks
around my house, to muse or to be irresponsible as I
please, and as you say, to go wool-gathering … That,
sir, is for me the greatest pleasure, to which I can
imagine nothing superior in this life, or even in the
next.

JEAN JACQUES ROUSSEAU

☞   ENERGY
       IDLERS
       INDOLENCE
       LAZINESS

IDLERS

I have seen slower people than I am – and more deliberate ... and even quieter, more listless, and lazier people than I am. But they were dead.

MARK TWAIN

✪

The great secret society of layabouts, enjoying the scorn of a world which works too hard.

PAUL MORAND

✪

They had no intention of going anywhere in particular; they wanted to see nothing, they wanted to know nothing, they wanted to learn nothing, they wanted to do nothing. They wanted only to be idle.

CHARLES DICKENS

✪

The idler will not be heard among the dogmatists. He will have a great and cool allowance for all sorts of people and opinions.

ROBERT LOUIS STEVENSON

Some are born lazy, some have idleness thrust upon
them, and others spend a great deal of effort creating
a careless nonchalance.

BERYL DOWNING

✪

The idler is naturally censorious; those who attempt
nothing themselves think every thing easily
performed.

SAMUEL JOHNSON

✪

How various his employments whom the rest of the
world calls idle!

WILLIAM COWPER

✪

The truly enlightened man has no learning, no
virtue, no accomplishments, no fame.

CHUANG-TSE

✪

For ye be lyke the sweynte cat
That wolde have fissh; but wostow what?
He wolde nothing wete his clowes.

GEOFFREY CHAUCER

The Importance of Being Idle

There is no dearer lover of lost hours
                                    Than I.
I can be idler than the idlest flowers;
                                    More idly lie
Than noonday lilies languidly afloat,
And water pillowed in a windless moat,
And I can be
Stiller than some grey stone
That hath no motion known.
It seems to me
That my still idleness doth make my own
All magic gifts of joy's simplicity.

S Weir Mitchell

✪

Idling has always been my strong point. I take no
credit to myself in the matter – it is a gift. Few
possess it. There are plenty of lazy people and plenty
of slowcoaches, but a genuine idler is a rarity.

Jerome K Jerome

✪

The need for laziness becomes overpowering in all of
us from time to time. We long for a vacation. We
want to recuperate from work. Well, there are a few
sensible people. They go off into a corner somewhere
and are as lazy as can be.

Dr Wilhelm Stekhel

See   **IDLENESS**
           LOAFING
           SLUGGARDS

IMAGINATION

Imagination is more important than knowledge.

ALBERT EINSTEIN

☞   CREATIVITY
           INVENTIVENESS

'Exams begin tomorrow, and I still don't know anything,' my friend complained.

'Don't worry,' I said, reassuringly. 'Knowledge is overrated.'

'But surely I need to know something?' he asked.

'You must not rely on knowledge,' I said. 'Knowledge is acquired only as a result of endeavour. It is something deliberately sought, and it is gained only by means of toil. Imagination, the product of idleness, is more important.'

'I can't rely on imagination alone.'

'You must,' I replied. 'One's imagination roams free and undirected. It is active without toil. The laborious search for knowledge will destroy one's powers of imagination. One's creative faculties will be buried beneath a dusty pile of old facts. Knowledge is stifling, but imagination is liberating.'

'I see your point, I suppose,' my friend said.

'Imagination, you see, produces originality,' I continued, 'but knowledge is simply the recycling of other people's tired old ideas.'

'And yet,' he protested, 'for the last three years you've consistently recycled my essays whilst pretending, extremely convincingly, I might add, that they are your original work.'

'Hence this reliance on my powers of imagination now,' I remarked, nonchalantly.

INDOLENCE

My indolence ... has sunk into grosser sluggishness ... A kind of strange oblivion has overspread me, so that I know not what has become of the last year.

SAMUEL JOHNSON

✪

Alas! The hours we waste is work
And similar inconsequence.
Friends, I beg you do not shirk
Your daily task of indolence.

DON MARQUIS

✪

Majestic indolence.

WILLIAM WORDSWORTH

☞   IDLENESS
        LAZINESS
        LOAFING

'IDLENESS,' SAID MY FRIEND, RECITING THE Earl of Chesterfield's famous dictum, 'is only the refuge of weak minds, and the holiday of fools.'

'Quotation is the refuge of weak minds,' I replied, refilling his glass with port.

'Then your mind is the weakest in town,' my friend retorted.

'Of course,' I said, languidly. 'But do not expect me to take Chesterfield's word for it. He was wrong. His claim is utterly false.' I stopped speaking for a moment and attempted to locate my matches.

'The words may be Chesterfield's, but the sentiment is mine,' he replied. He took his lighter from his pocket and passed it to me.

'And unoriginal sentiments are the holiday of fools,' I said. 'Idleness, on the other hand, is the citadel of strong minds, the fortress of vigorous intellects.' I lit my pipe. 'When we have nothing to do,' I continued, 'we cannot avoid thinking about things. When we are idle, our minds leap into action.' I waited for a reply, but my friend seemed to have dozed off in his chair. Must have been the port, I suppose.

INDUSTRY

Industry is the root of all ugliness.

OSCAR WILDE

★

The tempo of modern industrial life forbids glorious and magnificent idling.

LIN YUTANG

☞ BUSINESS
WORK

INTELLECTUALS

All intellectual improvement arises from leisure.

SAMUEL JOHNSON

✪

To do nothing at all is the most difficult thing in the world, the most difficult and the most intellectual.

OSCAR WILDE

✪

Laziness implies a lot of intelligence. It is the normal healthy attitude of a man with nothing to do.

SIR HENEAGE OGLIVIE

✪

Thinkers don't work, and workers can't think.

ENGLISH PROVERB

✪

Ease and relaxation are profitable to all studies. The mind is like a bow, the stronger by being unbent.

BEN JONSON

The Importance of Being Idle

Until we begin to understand that there is a leisure
which does not mean an easy sauntering through life,
but a special form of activity, employing all our
faculties, and training us to the adequate reception
of whatever is most valuable in literature and art ...
we are still as remote as ever from the serenity of
intellectual accomplishment.

AGNES REPPLIER

✪

We must be indulgent to the mind, and from time to
time we must grant it the idleness that serves as its
food and strength.

SENECA

✪

Scholarship is idle – apparently useless – questioning,
but it is also the epitome of purposeful work –
method and composition.

RUTH FOX

✪

Idleness, but idleness full of thought, and alive to
every impression.

MAURICE DE GUÉRIN

No man is born with the urge to work, for you cannot work and think.

HEATHCOTE WILLIAMS

✪

The idler, though sluggish, is yet alive, and may sometimes be stimulated to vigour and activity. He may descend into profoundness, or tower into sublimity; for the diligence of the idler is rapid and impetuous ... But these vehement exertions of intellect cannot be frequent.

SAMUEL JOHNSON

☞   CREATIVITY
      CURIOSITY
      WISDOM

INVENTIVENESS

I don't think necessity is the mother of invention. Invention arises directly from idleness, possibly also from laziness. To save oneself trouble.

AGATHA CHRISTIE

✪

Leisure is the mother of discovery.

MICHAEL FOSTER

   CREATIVITY
        IMAGINATION

JEROME K JEROME

Jerome Klapka Jerome (1859-1927) left school at the age of 14 and suffered a number of very short careers before he took up that idler's stand-by: writing. He is best remembered for his novel *Three Men in a Boat*, a semi-autobiographical tale of three indolent young men on a boating excursion up the river Thames. Jerome also wrote *The Idle Thoughts of an Idle Fellow*, a collection of essays about the easy life. In 1892 Jerome founded a monthly literary magazine which he named *The Idler* after Dr Johnson's column of the same name. The best writers of the age contributed: Mark Twain, Robert Louis Stevenson, Guy de Maupassant, Arthur Conan Doyle, and Rudyard Kipling, to name but a few.

Jerome wrote both for and about the newly literate middle-class workers, created by Victorian educational reform, who slaved in large cities as scribners and petty clerks. They were the first generation to be subjected *en masse* to the mundane world of 'office life' – the ranked desks and gloomy 'feeding pens' that we know so well today. Jerome's humorous anti-work ethos offered solace to many a weary worker both then and ever since.

☞   LITERATURE

SAMUEL JOHNSON

Samuel Johnson's praise for idleness is scattered throughout this little book. Most of these quotations are taken from his periodical *The Idler*, which was published between 1758 and 1760, and the rest have been taken from Boswell's Life of Johnson. Samuel Johnson was, by he own admission, a very idle fellow, and he was proud to admit it, ridiculing those who made disparaging remarks about idleness. And Boswell was a supreme idler too, or so Dr Johnson said.

During the course of a dinner at a coaching inn, a woman told Dr Johnson that she had done her best to educate her children, and, particularly, that she had never allowed them to be idle.

'I wish,' replied Dr Johnson, 'I wish, Madam, you would educate me too; for I have been an idle fellow all my life.'

'I am sure, Sir,' said she, 'you have not been idle.'

'Nay, Madam, it is very true; and that gentlemen there,' said Johnson, pointing to Boswell, 'has been idle. He was idle at Edinburgh. His father sent him to Glasgow, where he continued to be idle. He then came to London, where he has been very idle; and now he is going to Utrecht, where he will be as idle as ever.'

KENKO YOSHIDA

I wonder what feelings inspire a man to complain of
'having nothing to do'. I am happiest when I have
nothing to do.

KENKO YOSHIDA

The Buddhist monk Kenko Yoshida (1283-1350) wrote
a collection of short observations entitled *Tsurezuregusa*,
which translates into English as 'Essays in Idleness'. In its
opening chapter he wrote: 'What a strange, demented
feeling it gives me when I realise I have spent whole days
before this ink-stone with nothing better to do, jotting
down at random whatever nonsensical thoughts have
entered my head.' Kenko was, perhaps, a little self-
deprecating: *Essays in Idleness* is certainly not a collection
of nonsensical thoughts. Rather, as the scholar Donald
Keene has explained, it is 'a work of timeless relevance, a
splendid example of the Japanese meditative style'.

It is interesting to note that Kenko never compiled his
writings himself. Instead, he recorded his thoughts on
scraps of paper and pasted these onto the walls of his
cottage. After his death, this unusual wallpaper was
painstakingly removed and edited to produce the two
hundred and forty-three chapters of *Essays in Idleness*.

As a Buddhist, Kenko was aware of the importance of
contemplation, meditation, and withdrawal from the

world. 'Even if a man has not yet discovered the path of enlightenment,' he wrote, 'as long as he removes himself from his worldly ties, leads a quiet life, and maintains his peace of mind by avoiding entanglements, he may be said to be happy, at least for the time being.'

☞   BUDDHISM

PAUL LAFARGUE

For the proletariat to realise its own strength it must discover its natural instincts and proclaim that the right to leisure is a thousand times more sacred and noble than the Rights of Man advocated by the metaphysical lawyers of the middle-class revolution.

PAUL LAFARGUE

Paul Larfargue was a Cuban-born Frenchman who became the son-in-law of Karl Marx and founded the French Marxist Party. In 1880 he wrote a pamphlet called *Le Droit à la Paresse* ('The Right to be Lazy'), which became his most popular and enduring piece of writing. In it he emphasised the 'virtues of idleness' and condemned the 'exhausting' labour to which the proletariat were subjected by the capitalist system. The essay was extremely sophisticated: Larfargue discussed the many church-related holidays in the Middle Ages; the shorter working week of the ancien regime; and writers like Virgil, Rabelais and Cervantes who praised leisure. He offered plenty of examples of the intellectual and creative attainments reached by those who, like the Greeks, taught 'a contempt for work'. The essence of his cry was impassioned and emotional:

'O idleness, take pity on our long misery! O idleness, mother of the arts and noble virtues, be the salve of our human anguish!'

LAZINESS

Laziness is the one divine fragment of godlike existence left to man from paradise.

SCHLEGEL

✪

Gain a moment's rest for dreamy laziness.

JEROME K JEROME

✪

Let us be lazy in everything, except in loving and drinking, except in being lazy.

GOTTHOLD EPHRAIM LESSING

I could have a job, but I'm too lazy to choose it;
I have got land, but I'm too lazy to farm it.
My house leaks; I'm too lazy to mend it.
My clothes are torn; I'm too lazy to darn them.
I have got wine, but I'm too lazy to drink;
So it's just the same as if my cup were empty.
I have got a lute, but I'm too lazy to play;
So it's just the same as if it had no strings.
My family tells me there is no more steamed rice;
I want to cook, but I'm too lazy to grind.
My friends and relatives write me long letters;
I should like to read them, but they're such a bother
to open.
I have always been told that Hsi Shu-yeh
Passed his whole life in absolute idleness.
But he played his lute and sometimes worked at his
forge;
So even he was not as lazy as me.

PO CHÜ-I, 811 AD

☞   IDLENESS
       INDOLENCE
       SLEEP

LEISURE

If you are losing your leisure, look out! You may be losing your soul.

LOGAN PEARSALL SMITH

✪

Only those who take leisurely what the people of the world are busy about can be busy about what the people of the world take leisurely.

CHANG CH'AO

✪

If I am doing nothing, I like to be doing nothing to some purpose. That is what leisure means.

ALAN BENNETT

✪

Some men are born to leisure, some seek leisure, and some have leisure thrust upon them.

H J HEXTER

☞　　　RELAXATION

LETTERS

On the whole, if one answers letters promptly, the result is about as good or as bad as if one had never answered them at all. After all, nothing happens, and while one may have missed a few good appointments, one may have also avoided a few unpleasant ones. Most of the letters are not worth answering if you keep them in your drawer for three months. Reading them three months afterwards, one might realise how utterly futile and what a waste of time it would have been to answer them all.

LIN YUTANG

LIFE

The good people conceived of life as a state of perfect repose and idleness, disturbed at times by unpleasant accidents, such as illness, loss of money, quarrels, and work. They endured work as a punishment laid upon our forefathers, but they could not love it and avoided it whenever they could, believing it was possible and right to do so.

IVAN GONCHAROV

✪

Term, holidays, term, holidays, till we leave school, then work, work, work till we die.

C S LEWIS

✪

Let your boat of life be light, packed with only what you need – a homely home and simple pleasures, one or two friends, worth the name, someone to love and someone to love you, a cat, a dog, and a pipe or two, enough to eat and enough to wear, and a little more than enough to drink; for thirst is a dangerous thing.

JEROME K JEROME

For the time that a man may call his own, that
is his life.

CHARLES LAMB

✪

Death is the end of life; ah, why
Should life all labour be?

ALFRED, LORD TENNYSON

✪

To an impartial estimate it will seem clear that many
of the wisest, most virtuous, and most beneficent
parts that are to be played upon the Theatre of Life
are filled by gratuitous performers, and pass, among
the world at large, as phases of idleness.

ROBERT LOUIS STEVENSON

✪

Life is one long process of getting tired.

SAMUEL BUTLER

✪

Work to survive, survive by consuming, survive to
consume: the hellish cycle is complete.

RAOUL VANEIGEN

A whole lifetime of horrid industry.

WALTER BAGEHOT

✪

Life is lived in too great a hurry for the capture of joy in its passing.

GILBERT QUIN

✪

We are being jolted along from moment to moment. Every instant is a newcomer indifferent to the one before. Contemplation of action in the very instant of action is needed for the full enjoyment of life. However fast we run, we cannot overtake ourselves. However much we vary our experiences, we merely zigzag down the single track of one-dimensional time stretching from birth to death. However painfully we twist, we cannot catch the tail of the slipping instant. This is our common plight. Idleness is the protest. This is where we go on strike.

WILLIAM GERHARDI

✪

All this absurd talk about making your way in life never took me in. Why make your way? There are thousands of ways already. Enough to distract any man but an Idler, and drive him off his head.

WALTER RAYMOND

Life is just one damned thing after another.

ELBERT HUBBARD

✪

Life was divided, in his opinion, into two halves: one
consisted of work and boredom – these words were
for him synonymous – and the other of rest and
peaceful good humour.

IVAN GONCHAROV

✪

Ease, idleness, amusement, recreation and sleep are
among the most pleasant things in life.

ARISTOTLE

✪

Life is something to do when you can't get to sleep.

FRAN LEBOWITZ

✪

My life is one demd horrid grind.

CHARLES DICKENS

✪

Life is a perpetual toothache.

LOGAN PEARSALL SMITH

They had never heard of life being hard, of men being overwhelmed with anxious worries, rushing about from place to place, or devoting themselves to continuous, never-ending labour ... they did not think that life could consist in striving for some distant aim ... Life flowed on like a quiet river, and all that remained for them was to sit on the bank watching the inevitable events that presented themselves, uncalled for, to everyone in his turn.

IVAN GONCHAROV

☞ DEATH
WORK

LIN YUTANG

I have a reputation for lolling. Now there are many lollers among my friends and acquaintances, but somehow I have acquired a special reputation for lolling, at least in the Chinese literary world.

LIN YUTANG

The Chinese writer and philosopher Lin Yutang (1895-1976) lived in the USA for a great deal of his life. Much of his work is written in a light-hearted attempt to examine the contrasting lifestyles of China and America by highlighting the antagonistic philosophies of East and West. The oriental attitude, he argued, was sleepy and carefree, while a fanatical obsession with work dictated the American way of life. The following passage, taken from his treatise *The Importance of Living*, epitomises his tongue-in-cheek style:

'Sometimes a prophetic vision comes to me, a beautiful vision of a millennium when Manhattan will go slow, and when the American 'go-getter' will become an Oriental loafer. American gentlemen will float in skirts and slippers and amble on the side-walks of Broadway with their hands in their pockets, if not with both hands stuck in their sleeves in the Chinese fashion ... Someone will be brushing his teeth outside his shop-front, talking the while placidly with his neighbours, and once in a while a scholar will sail by with a limp volume rolled up and tucked away in his sleeve. Lunch counters will be abolished, and people will be lolling and lounging in soft, low armchairs in an Automat, while others will have learned the art of killing a whole afternoon in some café. A glass of orange juice will last half an hour, and people will learn to sip wine by slow mouthfuls, punctuated by delightful, chatty remarks, instead of swallowing it at a gulp. Registration in a hospital will be abolished, 'emergency wards' will be unknown, and patients will exchange their philosophy with their doctors. Fire engines will proceed at a snail's pace, their staff stopping on the way to gaze at and dispute over the number of passing wild geese in the sky.'

LITERATURE

Writers of course are the mavens of sloth ... Idle dreaming is often the essence of what we do.

THOMAS PYNCHON

✪

It is in our idleness, in our dreams, that the submerged truth sometimes comes to the top.

VIRGINIA WOOLF

✪

Oh! the only part of life that matters is contemplation. When everybody understands that as clearly as I do, they will all start writing. Life will become literature. Half of humankind will devote itself to reading and studying what the other half has written. And contemplation will be the main business of the day.

ITALO SVEVO

✪

What no wife of a writer can ever understand is that he's working when he is staring out the window.

BURTON ROSCOE

Persons devoted to mere literature commonly become devoted to mere idleness.

WALTER BAGEHOT

✪

Although professional writers may affirm that the aspirations of literature are lofty and transcendental, there is no doubt it has another more vulgar and immediate aim: to fill the idle moments of hypothetical readers ... When are we going to read, if not in a moment of idleness?

JOAN FUSTER

✪

People say that life is the thing, but I prefer reading.

LOGAN PEARSALL SMITH

✪

Most of my writing has been an instinctive pleasure, a playful impulse, as in running down a grassy slope or exploring a woodland path.

GEORGE SANTAYANA

When lately I retired to my house I resolved that, in so far as I could, I would cease to concern myself with anything except the passing in rest and retirement of the little time I still have to live. I could do my mind no better service than to leave it in complete idleness to commune with itself, to come to rest, and to grow settled ... But I find that on the contrary, like a runaway horse, it is a hundred times more active on its own behalf than it ever was for others. It presents me with so many chimeras and imaginary monsters, one after another, without order or plan, that, in order to contemplate their oddness and absurdity at leisure, I have begun to record them in writing, hoping in time to make my mind ashamed of them.

MICHEL DE MONTAIGNE

❂

Authors – gentlemen who lounge about on sofas, drink sherry, and smoke pipes.

IVAN GONCHAROV

123

The Importance of Being Idle

Sloth in writers is always a symptom of an acute inner conflict, especially that laziness which renders them incapable of doing the thing which they are most looking forward to. The conflict may or may not end in disaster, but their silence is better than the overproduction which must so end and slothful writers such as Johnson, Coleridge, Greville, in spite of the nodding poppies of conversation, morphia and horse-racing, have more to their credit than Macaulay, Trollope or Scott. To accuse writers of being idle is a mark of envy or stupidity.

CYRIL CONNOLLY

☞ DICKENS, CHARLES
EICHENDORFF, JOSEPH VON
JEROME K. JEROME
OBLOMOV
MORE, SIR THOMAS
POETRY
STEVENSON, ROBERT LOUIS
TWAIN, MARK
WHITMAN, WALT
WILDE, OSCAR

LOAFING

I hope you will not so far expose yourself as to ask,
who was the founder of loafers. Know you not,
ignorance, that there never was such a thing as the
origin of loaferism? We don't acknowledge any
founder. There have always been loafers as there
were in the beginning, are now, and ever shall be –
having no material difference.

WALT WHITMAN

✪

Loafing is the Science of living without trouble.

BARRY PAIN

✪

When I have been in a dreamy, musing mood, I have
sometimes amused myself with picturing out a
nation of loafers. Only think of it! An entire loafer
kingdom! How sweet it sounds! Repose, – quietude, –
roast duck, – loafer. Smooth and soft are the terms
on our jarred tympanums.

WALT WHITMAN

The Importance of Being Idle

Loafing needs no explanation and is its own excuse.

CHRISTOPHER MORLEY

✪

It is better to have loafed and lost than never to have loafed at all.

JAMES THURBER

☞ ENERGY
IDLENESS
LAZINESS
WHITMAN, WALT

LOTUS-EATERS

Those who ate the honey-sweet fruit of the lotus tree lost any wish to bring back news or to return. All they now wanted was to stay with the Lotus-Eaters, to browse on the lotus fruit, forgetful of their homeward way.

HOMER'S ODYSSEY

In Greek mythology, the Lotus-Eaters (Lotophagi) were an idle tribe of people who lived on the coast of North Africa. They ate nothing but the delectable fruit of the lotus tree, which made them forget the past and live lethargically in contented idleness. In Homer's *Odyssey*, when Odysseus landed on their coast, some men from his advance guard sampled the lotus fruit, forgot their homes and families, and had to be carried back to the ships by their companions. Alfred, Lord Tennyson retold the story in his poem 'The Lotus-Eaters' (1832).

☞   ANCIENT GREECE
        SHANGRI-LA

WHILST LYING AWAKE IN BED ONE DAY LAST summer, I was annoyed by some rather inconsiderate knocking on my front door. I tried to ignore it, but to no avail. The knocking continued. Eventually I got out of bed and went to open the door.

A friend of mine strolled in.

'I hope it's important,' I said. 'I was in bed.'

'In bed?' he repeated, incredulously. 'But it's five o'clock in the afternoon. And it's a lovely day outside. I do hope this isn't a ludicrously early night.'

'It's nothing of the sort,' I said, defensively. 'I was simply lying in bed.'

'Why? What use is that?' He looked bewildered.

'Lying awake in bed' I said, breaking into a fit of pedagogy, 'is a highly productive activity. It enables one to plan the day ahead.'

'But there isn't much day ahead,' my friend objected. 'It's almost the evening now, you know.'

'Don't quibble,' I said. 'You would condemn my decadence if I said that I was considering the long night ahead.'

'Do I always condemn your decadence? I must seem so staid. Anyway, I refuse to believe that this sluggish inactivity can be as beneficial as you claim.'

'It's not mere inactivity,' I said. 'It's contemplation. It enables one to untangle any difficulties that one may meet, and to anticipate any obstacles that one may encounter.' I wanted to say more, but I was feeling too listless to speak.

'Don't be so melodramatic,' my said friend, laughing. 'An empty decanter and an empty pipe are the only difficulties that you are likely to encounter in life. And neither of these obstacles requires much in the way of forward-planning.'

LOVE

My ideal is to be idle and love a plump young girl.

ANTON CHEKHOV

✪

Love is born in idleness and, once born, by idleness is fostered.

OVID

✪

A grande passion is the privilege of people who have nothing else to do. That is the one use of the idle classes of a country.

OSCAR WILDE

☞ MARRIAGE
SEX

LYING IN BED

Lying down was not for Ilya Ilyitch either a necessity
as it is for a sick or a sleepy man, or an occasional
need as it is for a person who is tired, or a pleasure as
it is for a sluggard; it was his normal state. When he
was at home – and he was almost always at home –
he was lying down, and invariably in the same room.

IVAN GONCHAROV

✪

The happiest part of a man's life is what he passes
lying awake in bed in the morning. I have, all my life
long, been lying in bed till noon, yet I tell all young
men, and tell them with great sincerity, that nobody
who does not rise early will ever do any good.

SAMUEL JOHNSON

✪

It is amazing how few people are conscious of the
importance of the art of lying in bed ... in my
opinion, nine-tenths of the world's most important
discoveries, both scientific and philosophical, are
come upon when the scientist or philosopher is
curled up in bed.

LIN YUTANG

The Importance of Being Idle

Give me a bed and a book and I am happy.

Logan Pearsall Smith

✪

Lying in bed would be an altogether perfect and supreme experience if only one had a coloured pencil long enough to draw on the ceiling.

G K Chesterton

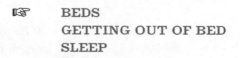 BEDS
GETTING OUT OF BED
SLEEP

MANKIND

The cardinal difference between man and the bird or beast is that one engages in a more or less voluntary frenzy of industry while the other is content to live in an idleness coloured only by an occasional quarrel.

GILBERT QUIN

✪

I am sure that indolence, indefeasible indolence, is the true state of man, and business the invention of the Old Teaser, who persuaded Adam's Master to give him an apron and set him ahoeing.

CHARLES LAMB

✪

It has been found hard to describe man by an adequate definition. Some philosophers have called him a reasonable animal; but others have considered reason as a quality of which many creatures partake. He has been termed likewise a laughing animal; but it is said that some men have never laughed. Perhaps man may be more properly distinguished as an idle animal; for there is no man who is not sometimes idle.

SAMUEL JOHNSON

All nature loafs, while man alone works for a living.

LIN YUTANG

☞ LIFE
WORK

MARRIAGE

When you see what some girls marry, you realise how they must hate to work for a living.

HELEN ROWLAND

☞ LOVE
SEX

MELANCHOLY

Melancholy has ceased to be an individual phenomenon, an exception. It has become the class privilege of the wage earner, a mass state of mind that finds its cause wherever life is governed by production quotas.

GÜNTER GRASS

☞ LIFE
WORK

MONASTICISM

The saints and holies of most religions tended to be those who sat around all day making a virtue of inactivity. Monks standing about in friaries contemplating mortality are, in anyone's book, dossers. The Buddhist in deep trance is the equivalent of the bad morning riser, while the hermit who spends forty years at the top of a pillar in the desert simply has a bad attitude to work – nothing a good kicking wouldn't sort out.

ARMANDO IANNUCCI

Throughout history, monks have been the torch-bearers for the noble art of idling. The monastic life of prayer, meditation and contemplative reading survived wave after wave of invading barbaric thugs to preserve learning through the dark ages. The Rule of St Benedict – the monastic daily timetable – divided the day into periods of simple work, community prayer and lectio divinia, a contemplative reading of the scriptures. Ideally, three hours every day are allotted to each task. Three hours of simple work, three hours of prayer and meditation, and three hours of reading. To put it another way, that's three hours of easy work and six hours of religious idling. And that's just nine hours out of every twenty-four – the other fifteen are the monk's free time, to read, to loaf, to relax, to sleep. For centuries the monk lived an easy life.

135

In the sixteenth century, Simon Fish, a London lawyer, wrote a work called *The Supplication for Beggars* in which he claimed that no one gave money to idle beggars any more because it had all been appropriated by idle monks. The monks, he claimed, had conned everyone and got all this cash on false pretences. Most people paid monks to pray for them after their death in order to reduce the amount of time they would have to spend in purgatory – the holding bay in which people were punished before reaching heaven. Imagine a kind of after-life insurance. But Simon Fish pointed out that the Church had made up all this nonsense about purgatory – it wasn't mentioned once in the Bible. It was all a big con trick to get money.

Unfortunately for English monks, in 1536, Henry VIII confiscated all monastic lands, and the rich bought this land from him at rock-bottom prices. With the dissolution of the monasteries, the English tradition of monastic idling came to a rather inglorious end. Thankfully, the idea of indolent monasticism was preserved throughout the rest of Europe by Catholics and maintained throughout the rest of world by religions other than Christianity.

☞ BUDDHISM
CHRISTIANITY
CONTEMPLATION

MONEY

Riches are chiefly good because they give us time.

CHARLES LAMB

✪

It is an exceedingly stupid person who will torment himself for the sake of worldly gain.

KENKO YOSHIDA

✪

To what end is wealth gathered if it be not for the acquisition of a leisured contentment?

GILBERT QUIN

✪

Honest poverty and a conscience torpid through virtuous inaction are more to me than corner lots and praise.

MARK TWAIN

✪

Wealth and idleness, which men count the first objects of desire ...

SALLUST

Idle gentlemen of private means, with fortunes large enough to support a life of enviable leisure, are few and far between. Hard work is bad, but most of us must endure some measure of work in order to survive. If we refuse to swim, we must at least tread water to keep our heads above the breadline. How is the idler of modest means to solve the financial problems created by his conscientious objection to work?

Simple. We must reintroduce patronage. Idling should rightly be viewed as one of the arts. The rich could sponsor the creative to be idle for society's benefit. The American performance artist Bob Powers called for this in April 1998. 'I would be thrilled,' he said, 'if I got a $25,000-a-year grant for the rest of my life. I don't want the money for any lofty goals. I want it just because I'm lazy and tired.'

SIR THOMAS MORE

The life of Sir Thomas More provides a perfect demonstration of the way in which idleness can lead to creativity. Between 1510 and 1515 Thomas More was an inordinately busy man. He had no spare time in which to pursue his own interests. He tried to write a history of Richard III, but was forced to leave it unfinished.

Everything changed in 1515, when Henry VIII sent More to the Netherlands to negotiate a trade treaty between England and Holland. The negotiations came to a standstill, and the Dutch negotiators went to consult their prince. During the summer of 1515, Thomas More found himself waiting in Holland until these Dutch intermediaries returned. As the historian H J Hexter has noted,

'That left More with very little to do ... it was nearly pure leisure – complete, indeed forced, freedom from all the ordinary obligations of a busy lawyer and a zealous father. More had the chance for the first time in years to think things over, to contemplate for days on end ... It was the kind of situation to snap the durable ties which imprison a man's fancy, which chain his imagination to the actual with the strong bonds of habit.'

More used this period of leisure to visit Peter Giles. They talked about many things in the pleasant summer of 1515. In particular they talked about the best ways to organise a nation. They tried to imagine the ideal state, a state in which no one would starve, a state with no injustice, a commonwealth in which people would care about the welfare of their countrymen. And from these discussions, *Utopia* was born. The work, a description of an imaginary island named Utopia, is a masterpiece surpassing almost all other works of its genre. He provided a vision of an entire society of Utopians. In this vision, work was limited to six hours a day so that people would have time to spend enjoying art and literature. This vision of idleness was the product of idleness – 'forced' idleness, as Hexter called it.

☞   **LITERATURE**
            PARADISE

NOBILITY

Idleness is an appendix to nobility.

ROBERT BURTON

✪

In the past, there was a small leisure class and a larger working class. The leisure class enjoyed advantages for which there was no basis in social justice; this naturally made it oppressive, limited its sympathies, and caused it to invent theories by which to justify its privileges.

BERTRAND RUSSELL

✪

Acquaintancewith the nobility, I could never keep up. It requires a life of idleness, dressing and attendance on their parties.

JOHN CAMPBELL

I have long been of the opinion that if work were such a splendid thing the rich would have kept more of it for themselves.

BRUCE GROCOTT

✪

Do nothing, be like a gentleman, be idle.

GEORGE CHAPMAN

The nobility of England, my lord, would have snored through the Sermon on the Mount.

ROBERT BOLT

✪

It has already been remarked that gentlemen do not work but this is only partly true, for their are certain occupations in which a gentleman can indulge. It is one of the conditions, however, that whatever he undertakes should have little chance of showing a satisfactory financial return.

DOUGLAS SUTHERLAND

Throughout history, the nobility endeavoured to be as idle as possible. They consistently sought to avoid hard work. The ruling classes lived a blissful life where work was no longer necessary for survival and where any activity was performed simply for its own sake. Their leisure was the primary index of their status. Of course, their indolent lifestyle was supported by the endless travails of countless peasants and serfs, but the divinely orchestrated social hierarchy never affected a nobleman's conscience.

A real nobleman delights in idleness and will object most strongly to work. What demonstrates this most clearly is the true English gentleman's distaste for 'new money'. In the aristocrat's eyes, the *arriviste* who has industriously 'worked' his way to an equal financial standing is the worst kind of creature imaginable. It is the very industry involved in acquiring his wealth that makes the *parvenu* so despicable. True nobility is part of an older contract and as outside the industrious loop of capitalism as any red-blooded communist.

But however rich the businessman may become, 'new money' will never be on a par with 'old money'. The late Alan Clark, himself a member of the landed squirearchy, made this perfectly clear. The worst thing he could find to say about fellow Conservative minister Michael Heseltine, whom Clark considered an impostor, was that he had 'bought' his furniture. Real gentlemen, you understand, inherit.

☞ CIVILISATION
PARLIAMENT

OBLOMOV

The Russian author Ivan Goncharov (1812-1891) wrote *Oblomov* in 1859. The story concerns an indolent Russian provincial landowner, named Ilya Ilyitch Oblomov, who lived in St. Petersburg. He is, without a doubt, the laziest man in Russian literature.

Oblomov's time was spent lying in bed in his room — a room, says Goncharov, 'where sleep and sloth reigned supreme'. When he was not in bed, he was to be found 'sitting dreamily in the easy-chair in his usual gracefully lazy attitude, not noticing what was happening around him or listening to what was being said.'

He had rejected a career so that 'he could give free play to his feelings and imagination' instead. So influential was the tale that the word 'oblomovism' entered the Russian language as a designation of habitual laziness.

☞   BARTELBEY THE SCRIVENER
        GORING, LORD
        RIP VAN WINKLE

OBLIGATIONS

No man, sir, is obliged to do as much as he can.

SAMUEL JOHNSON

☞   IDLENESS
        RIGHTS

PARADISE

Imagine some distant isle inhabited altogether by loafers. Of course, there is a good deal of sunshine, for sunshine is the loafer's natural element. All breathes peace and harmony. No hurry, or bustle, or banging, or clanging. Your ears ache no more with the din of carts; the noisy politician offends you not.

WALT WHITMAN

☞   MORE, SIR THOMAS
        SHANGRI-LA

PARLIAMENT

Arlington Stringham made a joke in the House of
Commons. It was a thin House, and a very thin joke;
something about the Anglo-Saxon race having a great
many angles. It is possible that it was unintentional,
but a fellow-member, who did not wish it to be
supposed that he was asleep because his eyes were
shut, laughed.

SAKI

✪

I was surprised to observe the very small attendance
usually in the House of Lords. Out of 573 peers, on
ordinary days only twenty or thirty. Where are they?
I asked. 'At home on their estates, devoured by
ennui, or in the Alps, or up the Rhine, in the Harz
Mountains, or in Egypt, or in India, on the Ghauts.'
But with such interests at stake, how can these men
afford to neglect them? 'O,' replied my friend, 'why
should they work themselves, when every man in
England works for them and will suffer before they
come to harm?'

RALPH WALDO EMERSON, 1853

A Parliament is nothing less than a big meeting of
more or less idle people.

WALTER BAGEHOT, 1867

When Emerson and Bagehot wrote these remarks in the
mid-nineteenth century, they were entirely correct.
Parliament met for a total of three or four months
each year. When Parliament met, the ruling classes
occasionally took up their places on the benches of the
House of Lords and snoozed, waking intermittently to
dine in sumptuous gentlemen's clubs. When the session
was over, they went back to their estates to snooze in
front of fires in their sumptuous drawing rooms and
well-stocked libraries. Hereditary peers at Westminster
are now a thing of the past and being a parliamentarian
is certainly no job for an idler today.

☞ NOBILITY

PATRIOTISM

I am an idler. A parasite. Unpatriotic.

S L LOWNDES

☞ CIVILISATION

PLANS

That the idler has some scheme cannot be doubted,
for to form schemes is the idler's privilege. But
though he has many projects in his head, he is now
grown sparing of communication, having observed
that his hearers are apt to remember what he forgets
himself; that his tardiness of execution exposes him
to the encroachments of those who catch a hint and
fall to work; and that very specious plans, after long
contrivance and pompous displays, have subsided in
weariness without a trial, and without miscarriage
have been blasted by derision.

SAMUEL JOHNSON

✪

Some are always in a state of preparation, occupied
in previous measures, forming plans, accumulating
materials, and providing for the main affair. These are
certainly under the secret power of idleness.

SAMUEL JOHNSON

OUR NATION SUFFERS FROM A LACK OF patriotism,' said my friend.

'In my opinion our nation suffers from a surplus of patriotism,' I replied. 'There's too much of the damned stuff.'

'How can you say such a thing?' he asked.

'You're idea of patriotism is outmoded,' I replied. 'Patriotism today must not be equated with the cheerful jingoism of our yesterdays. In the modern world, patriotism manifests itself in the form of a nationalistic work ethic. In these atheistic times, patriotism has ensured that sloth remains sinful.'

'Explain your theory.'

'Idleness is now an offence against the national economy rather than a sin against God,' I announced. 'As such, idleness is a sin against the nation. Hard work is patriotic, and the 'work-shy' can be denounced as traitors.'

'This is no fault of patriotism,' my friend objected.

'This development was accelerated by the Second World War,' I said, ignoring the interruption, 'when, in the name of patriotism, every man, woman and child was ordered to work long hours in munitions factories, and compelled to dig for victory.'

'For King and Country,' exclaimed my friend, 'and there was nothing wrong with that.'

'And as a result,' I said, ignoring the interruption again, 'idleness became a form of treachery, a means of harming the nation's chances of victory.'

'But this patriotic work ethic was itself an essential component of that victory,' replied my friend.

'If patriotism and idleness are incompatible,' I retorted, 'then we must reject our nation to preserve our civilisation.'

PLAY

All work and no play makes Jack a dull boy.

ENGLISH PROVERB

✪

Man is forgetting how to play. Yes, we have taught the masses that work is sacred, hard work. Now that the man of the mass is coming into his own he threatens to reimpose the belief we imposed on him. The men of no tradition 'dropped into history through a trapdoor' in a short space of 150 years were never taught to play, were never told that their work was 'sacred' only in the sense that it enabled their masters to play.

ALEXANDER TROCCHI

☞ CREATIVITY
IMAGINATION

PHILOSOPHY

An idle life is the life for me –
Idleness spiced with philosophy.

R BUCHANAN

✪

Philosophy began with the sense of boredom.

LIN YUTANG

Philosophy, said Wittgenstein, is 'language idling'. The philosopher, to paraphrase George Bernard Shaw, is an idler who kills time with study. Paul Virilio suggested that philosophy is the product of 'idle (often pointless) curiosity, born of the disappearance of physical effort once this becomes unnecessary.'

☞   **GREEK PHILOSOPHY**

POETRY

Idleness is the nurse of poets.

D'ARCY CRESSWELL

✪

… to articulate sweet sounds together
Is to work harder than all these, and yet
Be thought an idler by the noisy set
Of bankers, schoolmasters, and clergymen
The martyrs call the world.

WILLIAM BUTLER YEATS

Despite Yeats' claim to the contrary, all poets produce their verses as a result of idleness. In 1807 Byron called his first collection of poetry *Hours of Idleness* in appreciation of this fact. John Keats was once described while at university by a fellow-student as 'an idle, loafing fellow, always writing poetry'. The courtier poets of Elizabethan England produced all their best work as a result of idleness — a fact that disturbed them greatly because it disproved the Renaissance ideal of virtuous action. Wordsworth summed up this artistic tension between idleness and activity with the memorable phrase, 'A day / Spent in a round of strenuous idleness.'

☞   CREATIVITY
          IMAGINATION
          LITERATURE

PROTESTANT WORK ETHIC

Personally, I have nothing against work, particularly when performed quietly and unobtrusively, by someone else. I just don't happen to think it's an appropriate subject for an 'ethic'.

BARBARA EHRENREICH

✪

It has become an article of the creed of modern morality that all labour is good in itself – a convenient belief to those who live on the labour of others.

WILLIAM MORRIS

✪

The proverb says, jokingly, "either eat well or sleep well". In the present case the Protestant prefers to eat well, the Catholic to sleep undisturbed.

MARTIN OFFENBACHER

The Importance of Being Idle

The tradition of ascetic Protestantism is responsible for the belief that idleness is wrong. It was German sociologist Max Weber in his great work *The Protestant Ethic and the Spirit of Capitalism* who first identified Calvinism as the shadowy influence lurking behind the work ethic.

French theologian John Calvin (1509-64) taught the doctrine of predestination: that there was a distinct group of people whom God had chosen to go to heaven. This group – 'the elect' – had been chosen before they had been born. Those not chosen would be consigned to eternal damnation, and nothing they could do would change this.

At first you might believe that Calvin's doctrine seems more likely to produce idle men and women than toilers. If certain individuals are destined for heaven regardless of their behaviour on earth – and the rest are unable to overcome their damnation – there is little point in hard work on earth.

But, as Max Weber realised, Calvinists had a psychological problem – they did not know whether or not they were amongst the elect. They suffered from an inner-loneliness, an uncertainty about their status. So they tried to convince themselves that they had been chosen. Calvinists reasoned that those chosen by God would be successful on earth too. As a result, Calvinists became determined to succeed. They worked extremely hard to prove to themselves that they were amongst the elect.

The tenets of Calvinism had great implications – in particular that thrift, industry and hard work were forms of virtue and that business success was evidence of God's grace. The Calvinist ethic was ascetic, austere and rigorous in self-discipline. It produced workaholic individuals who were determined to become successful businessmen. As John Wesley, the leader of the Methodist movement in England at the end of the eighteenth-century, wrote:

'For religion must necessarily produce industry and frugality, and these cannot but produce riches. We must exhort all Christians to gain what they can and save all they can; that is, in effect, to grow rich.'

And because Calvinists were working so hard, they disliked the idea of idleness altogether. If they were not idle, they saw no reason why anyone else should be. For this reason, Calvinists attacked time-wasting, laziness and more sleep than was necessary – six hours at the most. It makes you feel tired just by thinking about it.

☞ CHRISTIANITY
   SEVEN DEADLY SINS

157

GILBERT QUIN

**Both in the purely domestic and in the international
spheres I feel that the importance of physical
comfort has received insufficient consideration.**

GILBERT QUIN

Gilbert Quin, the English essayist, wrote a number of
humorous articles promoting the joys of loafing. 'In
Defence of Idleness' saw Quin demolish the idea that
idleness was sinful: 'Exactly what is contained in the
definition of idleness,' he wrote, 'I have never been able
to determine, nor have I heard or read a satisfactory
explanation of the link between idleness and evil.'
Business and work, he concluded, were the causes of evil
in the world.

In 'The Tyranny of Time' he argued that 'time should
be the plaything of man, rather than his lord'. We should
not become slaves to time: instead, he argued, we must
relish the prospect of wasting time.

Quin emphasised the importance of physical comfort
in 'A Plea for Armchairs'. The choice of chairs, he
claimed, is a sure guide to character: 'The man who lowers
himself into an armchair with an exclamation of satis-
faction is one to whom a pipe may be offered without
fear of refusal.'

In his later essays, Quin's belief in idleness took on a pessimistic note as he dwelt on the worthlessness of human achievements: 'The progress of civilisation! What a wealth of human effort is held in that phrase – and what nothingness!'

RELAXATION

Workers of the world ... relax!

BOB BLACK

✪

Passions must have leisure to digest.

BISHOP HALL

✪

What a wonderfully unhurried feeling it is to live
even a single year in perfect serenity! If that is not
enough for you, you might live a thousand years and
still feel it was but a single night's dream.

KENKO YOSHIDA

✪

Lo! on the rural mossy bed
My limbs with careless ease reclin'd;
Ah, gentle sloth! indulgent spread
The same soft bandage o'er my mind.

WILLIAM SHENSTONE

The Importance of Being Idle

I would slip away and go throw myself alone into a boat that I rowed to the middle of the lake when the water was calm; and there, stretching myself out full-length in the boat, my eyes turned to heaven, I let myself slowly drift back and forth with the water, sometimes for several hours, plunged in a thousand confused, but delightful, reveries which, even without having any well-determined or constant object, were in my opinion a hundred times preferable to the sweetest things I had found in what are called the pleasures of life.

JEAN JACQUES ROUSSEAU

☞   IDLENESS
           LEISURE
           SUNBATHING

RETIREMENT

That happy age when a man can be idle with
impunity.

WASHINGTON IRVING

✪

Most people perform essentially meaningless work.
When they retire that truth is borne in upon them.

BRENDAN FRANCIS

☞ LIFE
WORK

REVOLUTION

For Satan finds some mischief still
For idle hands to do.

ISAAC WATTS

✪

A king can stand people's fighting, but he can't last
long if they start thinking.

WILL ROGERS

✪

Idleness overthrows all.

ROBERT BURTON

163

I WAS SITTING ON A WOODEN BENCH AMIDST the ragged foliage of the park, attempting to read a ponderous old tome, when an acquaintance of mine walked up and sat down beside me.

'I was thinking,' he said, 'about something you said the other day. You told me that everything worthy of note in human history was the product of idleness.'

'Indeed,' I replied, closing my book.

'Well, I've thought of an example that disproves your theory,' he said.

'Continue,' I demanded.

'Revolution is proof enough,' he said. 'That's not caused by idleness, is it? It's a strenuous activity. Storming the Bastille, and attacking the Winter Palace, and so on.'

'Sieges and battles are rarely undertaken in a slothful manner,' I agreed. 'But idleness has been the initial cause of every revolution. When the masses are idle, the position of the ruling classes becomes extremely precarious. Have you considered that?'

'Not really,' said my acquaintance, ruefully.

'Fortunately,' I continued, 'the rulers of society have considered it regularly. Governments have taken the initiative and endeavoured to keep people busy. The citizens will stay out of trouble for as long as they remain occupied by the bustling demands of toil. Busy men and women have no time to question the social and political order. Busy people have no time to organise revolutions.'

'I suppose you're right,' said my acquaintance.

'I am right,' I said. 'Revolutions are made by the idle. Let us take the French Revolution of 1789 as a suitable example. It was organised by political clubs, you know. These clubs were formed by loafers, by idlers. They were brought into being,' I continued, 'by men with plenty of spare time on their hands. Idle hands make idle work, as they say. Idlers have plenty of time to think about politics and society, about justice and injustice. They have enough time to entertain subversive ideas and revolutionary ambitions.'

I picked up my book and began leafing through its musty pages, waiting for a reply, but none was forthcoming. Instead my acquaintance lit a cigarette, deeming that to be sufficient in the circumstances.

RIGHTS

Every man has a right to live a life of idleness.

SENECA

✪

The right to laziness is one of the rights that sensible humanity will learn to consider as something self-evident. For the time being we are still in conflict with ourselves. We shun the truth. We look upon laziness as degrading. We still stand in too much awe of ourselves to be able to find the right measure. Our mothers' voices still ring in our ears: 'Have you done your lessons?'

DR WILHELM STEKHEL

Take away a man's right to idleness, and you enslave him in a life of merciless toil and exertion. When this violation of human rights is perpetrated on a full-time basis, it is known as slavery. When it is organised on a part-time basis, it is called capitalism.

☞   OBLIGATIONS
            SLAVERY

RIP VAN WINKLE

Rip Van Winkle was one of those happy mortals who take the world easy, and would rather starve on a penny than work for a pound.

WASHINGTON IRVING

When he wrote *Rip Van Winkle* in 1819, Washington Irving gave us one of American literature's most memorable loafers. Rip was a consummate idler. He had 'an insuperable aversion to all kinds of profitable labour.' If left to his own devices, Irving tells us, he 'would have whistled life away in perfect contentment.' But Rip's life was made a misery by his shrewish wife, who 'kept continually dinning in his ears about his idleness.'

When driven from his home by his wife's nagging, Rip would sit on a bench outside a tavern, talking to 'the sages, philosophers, and other idle personages of the village.' Here, in the company of his friends, Rip could relax: 'they used to sit in the shade through a long lazy summer's day, talking listlessly over village gossip, or telling endless sleepy stories about nothing.'

Often, however, his wife would come looking for him, so Rip would head for the hills for some peace and quiet. On one excursion up there, Rip met some peculiar little men playing ninepins. They offered him some brew from a keg, which made him feel very drowsy. Rip awoke and was extremely puzzled to find that his gun was rusty, that his dog was missing, and that he had grown an enormous white beard.

When he walked back to the village, he was surprised to find that he recognised no one, and that no one recognised him. After much confusion, he realised that he had been asleep for twenty years, during which time the American Revolution had occurred. Of course, this was all very distressing, but Rip was delighted to discover that his wife was dead.

☞ **BARTELBY THE SCRIVENER OBLOMOV**

LORD ROCHESTER

This very morning the King did publicly walk up and
down, and Rochester I saw with him as free as ever,
to the King's everlasting shame, to have so idle a
rogue his companion.

SAMUEL PEPYS

John Wilmot, the second Earl of Rochester, was
reckoned to be the idlest man in Restoration England.
He inherited his father's wealth and was given an annual
grant of £500 – a considerable sum at the time – by
Charles II. Rochester spent all his money on vast
quantities of wine, innumerable prostitutes, debauched
living, and ostentatious extravagance. He is remembered
for his scurrilous satires, his sexually explicit verses, and
his destructive alcoholism. During his lifetime, however,
he was notorious primarily on account of his idleness, as
Pepys's remark demonstrates. Rochester's verses remain
rallying cries for hedonists and libertines everywhere:

> Cupid and Bacchus my saints are;
> May drink and love still reign:
> With wine I wash away my cares,
> And then to love again.

☞ NOBILITY

169

ROUTINE

I confess that certain individuals appear to experience a queer delight in regular habits: in shaving at 7 AM and in saluting the office clock at 9 AM precisely. For my part I find such routine inimical to both health and temper.

GILBERT QUIN

☞ GETTING OUT OF BED
TIME
WORK

BERTRAND RUSSELL

The English philosopher Bertrand Russell (1872-1970) wrote a piquant essay in 1932 entitled 'In Praise of Idleness'. He claimed that there were only two kinds of work: 'first, altering the position of matter at or near the earth's surface relatively to other such matter; second, telling other people to do so.' While he championed common idling, he heaped opprobrium on society's idle landowners, denouncing them as men whose 'idleness is only rendered possible by the industry of others.'

Many of his insights are clever: 'the necessity of keeping the poor contented ... has led the rich, for thousands of years, to preach the dignity of labour, while taking care themselves to remain undignified.' But Russell's socialist standpoint becomes rather amusing when you remember that he was, to give him his full title, the third Earl Russell – an idle aristocrat through and through.

☞   NOBILITY
             SOCIALISM

SAKI

There won't be any great strain upon your powers of endurance; I promise you that you shan't have to play croquet, or talk to the Archdeacon's wife, or do anything that is likely to bring on physical prostration. You can just wear your sweetest clothes and a moderately amiable expression, and eat chocolate-creams with the appetite of a blasé parrot. Nothing more is demanded of you.

SAKI

Otherwise known as Hector Hugh Munro, Saki (1870-1916) is the genius of Edwardian literary brevity that brought us those idle young protagonists: Reginald, Clovis and Comus, lazy upper-crust aesthetes for whom the world is so tiresome, all they can do is smoke, lounge and issue the odd well-turned aphorism. Their world is one of relentless leisure, skipping between sleepy London clubs, afternoon tea in the drawing room and weekend parties in the country.

Much of Munro's own life was one of charmed low-key leisure. After being brought up by his aunts in Devon, he spent years touring Europe with his father, doing very little. He spent a year in the Burma police but the exertion was all too much for him and he soon returned to England for rest and recuperation after a bout of malaria. He settled in London working as a journalist and writer and led a refreshingly dull and routine life: rooms in Fitzrovia, an undistinguished club, and endless weekend house parties. A quiet man in public, he left the aphorisms to his fictional creations.

☞ LITERATURE

SCIENCE

It is not the accredited back-room boys who have made the notable discoveries in science, but idle men with vacant minds. Even Newton's sleep was a case of a golden apple falling into an idle slot.

WILLIAM GERHARDI

☞ ACHIEVEMENT

SENECA

The Roman philosopher and dramatist Seneca (4 BC–65 AD) wrote a lively little essay entitled *De Otio* ('On Idleness') in which he made a spirited plea for the life of philosophic leisure and contemplation. 'There are three kinds of life: one is devoted to pleasure, a second to contemplation, and a third to action,' he claimed. Rejecting the first and the third, he argued that 'contemplation is favoured by all.'

☞   CONTEMPLATION
      GREEK PHILOSOPHY

SEVEN DEADLY SINS

Many of the motives which make us sacrifice to toil
the innocent enjoyment of leisure are amongst the
most ignoble: pride, avarice, emulation, vainglory and
the appetite for power over others.

EVELYN WAUGH

Sloth is one of the Seven Deadly Sins. Its companions in
this regard are pride, anger, gluttony, envy, lust and greed.
It has been regarded as a vice for centuries. This is a cause
of considerable alarm for the more traditional idler who
still believes in hell and fiery demons. Don't worry, old
chap. There is nothing to fret about, I assure you.

The authoritative list of Seven Deadly Sins was
compiled by Pope Gregory the Great. Gregory, of
course, never used the word 'sloth'. He didn't speak
English. The word we translate as 'sloth' was a Greek
word that found its way into Latin – *acedia* in Greek, and
accidia in Latin. What does this word mean? When looking up a definition of an ancient Greek word, one must
turn to the deservedly famous *Greek Lexicon*, written by
the Reverend Henry Liddell and Robert Scott in the first
half of the nineteenth century. Liddell and Scott translate acedia as anguish and neglect. There's no mention of
sloth or idleness. The scholar of monasticism, John
Cassian, who died in 435 AD, described the way in which
the sin of acedia effected monks and hermits. He said

175

that it was like 'an intermittent fever' when a monk was overcome by 'dislike of the place, disgust with the room, and disdain and contempt of the monks'. The sin of acedia would make a monk 'lazy and sluggish' and he would begin to 'complain and sigh'.

Thomas Aquinas, who wrote during the thirteenth century AD, described acedia as 'an oppressive sorrow, which weighs upon a man's mind so that he wants to do nothing … this sorrow is always evil'. Peter Lombard, who wrote a discussion of Pope Gregory's list of sins, introduced the concept to his readers as 'acedia, which is the same thing as melancholy or mournfulness'. It was believed to be a sin because people were persisting in defiant sorrow in the face of God's good intentions.

As these opinions make clear, acedia was a condition that modern doctors would diagnose as clinical depression. Depression, not sloth, is the problem written about by Pope Gregory, John Cassian, Thomas Aquinas and Peter Lombard – and the word acedia was used to describe this problem. The symptoms of clinical depression are often a dislike of one's surroundings, a disdain for one's friends and a sorrowful inactivity – or, to put it another way, a sluggish melancholy. Acedia was regarded as a sin simply because no one understood anything much about anything even vaguely medical in those days. Acedia isn't idleness. Idleness was an occasional symptom of the problem, not the problem itself. The word 'sloth' is a gross mistranslation.

☞ CHRISTIANITY
HEAVEN
PROTESTANT WORK ETHIC
SLOTH

SEVEN SLEEPERS OF EPHESUS

The legend of the Seven Sleepers of Ephesus, a myth of Syrian origin, tells of seven young Christians who sought refuge in a cave in Ephesus in western Anatolia to escape the persecutions of the Roman emperor Decius. The emperor had the cave's entrance boarded up so that these seven subversives could starve to death. Instead the youngsters fell into a deep sleep that lasted for two centuries. When they awoke, they wandered into the city and, still youthful, were brought before the Emperor Theodosius II. Impressed by this supreme feat of lethargy, which he saw as proof of the doctrine of bodily resurrection, Theodosius ordered these somnolent youngsters to be venerated as saints.

☞ ENDYMION
SHANGRI-LA
SOMNUS

177

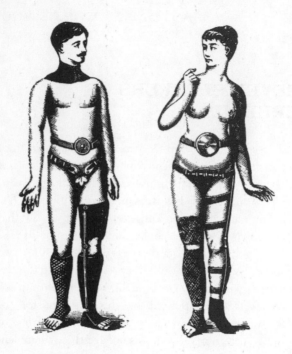

SEX

Intimacy with a woman involves too much exertion.

IVAN GONCHAROV

✪

It's not 'cause I wouldn't,
It's not 'cause I shouldn't,
And, Lord knows, it's not 'cause I couldn't,
It's simply because I'm the laziest gal in town.

COLE PORTER

Disciples of Tantric sex make grand claims for their peculiar hobby. Tantra, they declare, transports your sexuality from the plane of doing to the plane of being. Their ritual lovemaking is a participation in cosmic and divine processes transcending space and time, surpassing the duality of spirit and matter to recover a primal unity. I have my doubts about all this new age poppycock. I am sure that I'm not alone in regarding Tantric sex as a half-hearted excuse for idlers. "Can you put your hand on your heart and say that you are a sexual slacker?" Suzanne Moore once asked. Tantric sex provides an unconvincing answer: "I'm not a sexual slacker. I'm simply transporting my sexuality from the plane of doing to the plane of being."

☞   LOVE
        MARRIAGE

SHANGRI-LA

'Slacker,' explained Conway, 'is a slang word meaning a lazy fellow, a good-for-nothing. I wasn't, of course, using it seriously.'

Chang bowed his thanks for the information. He took a keen interest in languages and like to weigh a new word philosophically. 'It is significant,' he said after a pause, 'that the English regard slackness as a vice. We, on the other hand, should vastly prefer it to tension. Is there not too much tension in the world at present, and might it not be better if more people were slackers?

JAMES HILTON, LOST HORIZON

In 1933, a time of unrest throughout the world, James Hilton wrote the popular classic *Lost Horizon* introducing us to the comforting mythical land of Shangri-La. Secluded high in the Tibetan mountains, stumbled upon by a small group of westerners, it is a haven of eastern peace and tranquility, high culture and lazy learning; a harbour from a weary world where life moves at a very slow pace offering mental, emotional and physical contentment. A kind of magical utopia where all life's comforts are provided in profusion and, if you submit to the idler's life of easy contemplation, living for centuries is not beyond the bounds of possibility. Unfortunately, they no longer have any vacancies pending.

☞ LOTUS–EATERS
PARADISE

JOHN SKELTON

First I lay before them my Bible
And teach them how they should sit idle
To pick their fingers all the day long
So in their ear I sing them a song.

JOHN SKELTON

John Skelton (1460-1529) was appointed Poet Laureate and Orator Regius at the court of Henry VIII. For many years, however, he served as a priest in Norfolk. The verse above, taken from his play *Magnificence*, makes clear his idea that most clergymen did nothing but teach idleness by example.

☞ CHRISTIANITY
POETRY

SLEEP

I love sleep because it is both pleasant and safe to use. Sleep is death without the responsibility.

FRAN LEBOWITZ

✪

There is a school of thought that believes that sleep is for the night. You seem to be out to disprove them.

ALAN AYCKBOURN

✪

Harris said he didn't think George ought to do anything that would have a tendency to make him sleepier than he always was, as it might be dangerous. He said he didn't understand how George was going to sleep any more than he did now, seeing that there were only twenty-four hours in each day, summer and winter alike; but thought that if he did sleep any more he might just as well be dead, and so save his board and lodging.

JEROME K JEROME

✪

If I sleep, I sleep for myself; if I work, I know not for whom.

ITALIAN PROVERB

Come, Sleep! O Sleep, the certain knot of peace,
The baiting-place of wit, the balm of woe,
The poor man's wealth, the prisoner's release,
Th'indifferent judge between the high and low.

ALGERNON SIDNEY

✪

Blessings on him who invented sleep, the mantle that
covers all human thoughts, the food that appeases
hunger, the drink that quenches thirst, the fire that
warms cold, the cold that moderates heat, and lastly,
the general coin that purchases all things, the balance
and weight that equals the shepherd with the king,
and the simple with the wise.

MIGUEL DE CERVANTES

✪

Oh sleep! It is a gentle thing
Beloved from pole to pole.

SAMUEL TAYLOR COLERIDGE

✪

Sleep appears to be rather addictive. Many find that
they cannot do without it and will go to great lengths
to ensure its possession. Such people have been
known to neglect home, hearth, and even publishers'
deadlines in the crazed pursuit of their objective.

FRAN LEBOWITZ

183

The Importance of Being Idle

It's time for a little quiz. What do the Chernobyl and Three Mile Island nuclear disasters, the Challenger space shuttle explosion, the Exxon Valdez oil spill, and the sinking of the ferry the Herald of Free Enterprise all have in common? The answer is that they have all been blamed on human tiredness. Here's another question. When the USA's National Commission on Sleep Disorders presented its findings, how many Americans were said to be chronically affected? The answer, rather alarmingly, is forty million. That's an awful lot of tired people. And America is only part of the story. There is, it seems, a gigantic sleep debt across the industrialised world.

If we don't receive enough sleep, we suffer from poor functioning of the brain. Our powers of concentration become markedly diminished. Reasoning skills and linguistic coherence decrease. We become 'borderline retarded', as one recent scientific report put it. Falling an hour short of the desired nine hours can knock a point off your intelligence quotient, with two points lost if a further hour is skipped. Sleep deprivation forces the immune system to close down. Tired people are irritable, ineffectual, and prone to ill health. Hence the long list of man-made disasters in my initial question. Sleep is a resplendent thing. Take my advice, old chap. Stop reading this book and go back to bed forthwith.

☞ BEDS
GETTING OUT OF BED
LYING IN BED
HEALTH
RELAXATION

SLOTH

FAUSTUS: What art thou, the sixth?
SLOTH: I am Sloth; I was begotten on a sunny bank, where I have lain ever since – and you have done me great injury to bring me from thence. Let me be carried thither again by Gluttony and Lechery. I'll not speak another word for a king's ransom.

CHRISTOPHER MARLOWE

☞ SEVEN DEADLY SINS

SLUGGARDS

'Tis the voice of the sluggard, I heard him complain,
"You have waked me too soon, I must slumber again";
As the door on its hinges, so he on his bed,
Turns his side, and his shoulders, and his heavy head.
A little more sleep, and a little more slumber;
Thus he wastes half his days and his hours without
number;
And when he gets up, he sits folding his hands,
Or walks about saunt'ring or trifling he stands.

ISAAC WATTS

✪

'Sluggard' – why, it is a calling and vocation, it is a
career.

FYODOR DOSTOYEVSKY

☞ IDLERS
LOAFING

SOCIAL TRENDS

When the idle poor become the idle rich
You'll never know just who is who or who is which.

E Y HARBURG

✪

Modern methods of production have given us the
possibility of ease and security for all; we have chosen,
instead, to have overwork for some and starvation for
others. Hitherto we have continued to be as energetic
as we were before there were machines; in this we
have been foolish, but there is no reason to go on
being foolish forever.

BERTRAND RUSSELL

✪

Concerning the manner of work in civilised states,
these states are composed of three classes – a class
which does not even pretend to work, a class which
pretends to work but which produces nothing, and a
class which works, but is compelled by the other two
classes to do work which is often unproductive.

WILLIAM MORRIS

We are witnessing a worrying polarisation of our work
culture. People are working longer hours. They work

whilst travelling to their place of employment. They work through their lunch hour. And, at the end of the day, they take work home with them. Those who are employed are choosing to (or being insidiously coerced to) work harder and harder. If you are not working hard, you will end up not working at all.

There is an unprecedented level of job insecurity. Redundancies and short-term contracts have become an accepted part of our 'boom and bust' economy. Firms 'downsize' in times of economic difficulty. Profits must be maintained to keep the shareholders happy. The result is unhappiness in the workplace. Prospects have never been so bleak for the dedicated idler.

In the last three decades of the 20th century, subsisting on unemployment benefit was the obvious choice adopted by most idlers lacking a trust fund. Exchanging the dignity of labour for the joys of leisure turned the dole into a creative experience for many. But as governments makes it harder and harder for the casual idler to obtain benefits, he is forced to look elsewhere.

Downshifting seems to be the latest way out of the corporate feeding pens: swopping your stressful high-powered job-from-hell to return to something less finacially rewarding but more in keeping with your natural idle impulses: a freelance greetings-card poet perhaps?

☞ BUSINESS
INDUSTRY
WORK

SOCIALISM

It is the common error of Socialists to overlook the natural indolence of mankind.

JOHN STUART MILL

☞   INDOLENCE
           MANKIND

SOMNUS

In Roman mythology, Somnus was the god of sleep. The Greeks had christened him Hypnos, but the Romans, not content with plundering the Greek heavens, felt it their duty to rename everything they found therein. Somnus, in his Roman guise, was the son of Nox (night) and the father of the dream-god Morpheus. Somnus's home was in a dark cave in the distant west, where the sun never shone and all things were swathed in silence. Lethe, the river of forgetfulness, flowed nearby, and sleep-inducing poppies grew all around. Here Somnus spent his days in ceaseless slumber.

☞   ENDYMION
           7 SLEEPERS OF EPHESUS

ROBERT LOUIS STEVENSON

Perpetual devotion to what a man calls his business is only to be sustained by perpetual neglect of many other things.

ROBERT LOUIS STEVENSON

Robert Louis Stevenson (1850-1894), the great Scottish writer, achieved fame through his popular novels, of which *Treasure Island* and *The Strange Case of Dr Jekyll and Mr Hyde* are perhaps the most well-known. In 1876 the young Stevenson wrote 'An Apology for Idlers' in which he defended loafing, praised truancy, berated busy-bodies and denounced work.

☞ LITERATURE

STRESS

The demands of modern living ... are such that
almost everyone suffers from some sort of tension.
It is an occupational hazard. Most of us seem to be
constantly rushing to keep to a rigid time schedule,
and even those hours which are supposed to be for
leisure tend to get misused.

WILFRID NORTHFIELD

✪

To live with our emotions perpetually on the stretch,
and our minds always on the alert, is not to live, but
uselessly to waste the very fibre of our nervous being.

W C LOOSEMORE

☞   HEALTH

SUCCESS

Success is the one unpardonable sin against our
fellows.

AMBROSE BIERCE

☞   AMBITION
CAREERISTS

191

Shaking his head from side to side like a disappointed wildebeest, my friend walked through the door, stepped towards an armchair and sat down heavily. He held his head in his hands.

'I fear that I will be consumed by an apoplectic fit at any moment,' he said, dramatically.

'My dear fellow,' I said, 'whatever's the matter?'

'I've so much to do,' he replied, 'and so little time.'

'I can hardly believe that,' I replied. 'You never have anything to do.'

'I always have things to do,' he corrected, 'but I never actually do anything. So I haven't done the things I ought to have done, and I'm feeling a little tense as a result.'

'You should be more careful,' I advised. 'Stress is exceedingly bad for you.'

'Incorrect,' he replied. 'It's life that's exceedingly bad for you. The mortality rate is one hundred per cent.'

'I'm speaking in earnest,' I said.

'Do you have any aspirin?' he asked, quietly. 'I have a sore head.'

'That doesn't surprise me,' I replied. 'Stress can cause a great number of ailments, from headaches to heart attacks. Stress should be avoided at all costs.'

'I believe that life should be avoided at all costs.'

'And suicide is inexpensive,' I replied, 'which is probably just as well, as many are driven to it by bankruptcy.'

'It seems to be highly unfashionable to avoid life these

days,' my friend complained. 'Most stylish young things,' he continued, 'launch themselves with gusto into life's inviting embrace. But life is a demanding master. He will force you to rush around faster and faster to fulfil his requirements. And he does not forgive those who fail him. Stress, it seems, is the inevitable result.'

'How philosophical you are today,' I noted.

'The resigned reflections of the condemned man,' he added, darkly.

'Do cheer up,' I said. 'We must eliminate this nervous tension of yours.'

'You didn't answer me before,' my friend said. 'Do you have any aspirin?'

'It's no good treating the mere symptoms of stress,' I replied, 'because the basic cause will remain, and these stress-related disorders will return like the buds on the branches in spring.'

'What do you propose?'

'You must make a conscious effort to do far less than you think you can. If you are told to do a certain task within six hours, demand six months at the least. Spend your days in leisurely repose, gradually completing the task in hand, slowly but surely. You will find that stress becomes a thing of the past.'

'I can't do any less than I do already,' he replied, desperately. 'Now please, do you have any aspirin?'

SUNBATHING

What I like best is to lie whole mornings on a sunny bank ... without any object before me, neither knowing nor caring how time passes, and thus 'with light-winged toys of feathered idleness' to melt down hours to moments.

WILLIAM HAZLITT

✪

Just to sit in the Sun, to bask like an animal in the heat – this is one of my country recreations. And often I reflect what a thing after all it is, still to be alive and sitting here above all the buried people of the world, in the kind and famous sunshine.

LOGAN PEARSALL SMITH

☞   LESIURE
        RELAXATION

SUPPRESSION OF IDLENESS

In the Laws of Draco, those convicted of idleness
were put to death.

PLUTARCH

Idleness has often been a punishable offence. In the
Draconian Law Code (7th century BC), the punishment
was death. In Theodosian Law Code, the Romans made
sure that idleness remained illegal but they abandoned
the death penalty. The punishment for a man who was
'lazy and not to be pitied on account of any physical dis-
ability' was enslavement to the informer. So if you told
the authorities about a lazy man, he would become your
own personal slave for life. The same dastardly ruse was
contained within the Justinian Law Code.

This idea of personal enslavement was unexpectedly
resurrected in England in 1547 by the government of the
boy-king Edward VI. By the stipulations of this law,
if you refused to accept any work, however unpleasant
it may have been, and even if bread were offered in
payment instead of money, you were condemned and
enslaved to the man who had informed on you for a
period of two years. If you ran away, you would be
enslaved for life when recaptured. If you ran away again,
the punishment was death.

But the idea of enslavement to an individual as the
punishment for idleness was unusual after the decline of

the Roman Empire. Other punishments proved to be easier to enforce. An Act of Parliament passed in the reign of Henry VIII in 1530 made whipping the punishment for idleness, but the cat o' nine tails was not sufficient a deterrent, so in 1536 he made a new law. In the preamble to the law, Henry complained about 'the great number of idle people daily increasing throughout this Realm'. These people were spending their time 'in idleness ... to the high displeasure of Almighty God ... and extreme ruin, decay and impoverishment of this Realm'. The King said that his subjects must 'avoid that most abominable sin of idleness'. To ensure that his people would remain busy at all times, the King decided that the punishment for idleness would be mutilation or hanging – whichever you preferred.

☞   RIGHTS

TECHNOLOGY

Suppose that, at a given moment, a certain number of people are engaged in the manufacture of pins. They make as many pins as the world needs, working (say) eight hours a day. Someone makes an invention by which the same number of men can make twice as many pins as before. But the world does not need twice as many pins: pins are already so cheap that hardly any more will be bought at a lower price. In a sensible world, everybody concerned in the manufacture of pins would take to working four hours instead of eight, and everything else would go on as before. But in the actual world this would be thought demoralising. The men still work eight hours, there are too many pins, some employers go bankrupt, and half the men previously concerned in making pins are thrown out of work. There is, in the end, just as much leisure as on the other plan, but half the men are totally idle while half are still overworked. In this way, it is ensured that the unavoidable leisure shall cause misery all round instead of being a universal source of happiness. Can anything more insane be imagined?

BERTRAND RUSSELL

197

At present machinery competes against man. Under proper conditions machinery will serve man.

OSCAR WILDE

☞   SCIENCE

TIME

Time is a resource. Time runs out. The most basic problem facing any culture is the conservation and disbursement of time. Human time is measured in terms of human change. So the most flagrant time-wasting may minimise change and thus conserve time.

WILLIAM BURROUGHS

✪

I woke this morning out of dreams into what we call Reality, into the daylight, the furniture of my familiar bedroom – in fact into the well-known, often-discussed, but, to my mind, as yet unexplained Universe. Then I, who came out of Eternity and seem to be on my way thither, got up and spent the day as I usually spend it. I read, I pottered, I complained ... and I sat down punctually to eat the cooked meals that appeared at regular intervals.

LOGAN PEARSALL SMITH

You must have been warned against letting the golden hours slip by. Yes, but some of them are golden only because we let them slip.

J M Barrie

✪

Time is so obviously meant for wasting that in a perfectly sane world it would be unnecessary to emphasise the fact.

Gilbert Quin

✪

In idleness, eternity runs at right angles across every point, every distinct and separate moment on the line of one-dimensional time, perpetuating every single selected moment into eternity.

William Gerhardi

✪

While you sleep, your beard grows: this is time.

Joan Fuster

☞   LIFE

TOBACCO

Let us come out, and have a smoke. That wastes time just as well … Tobacco has been a blessing to us idlers. What the civil service clerks before Sir Walter's time found to occupy their minds with, it is hard to imagine. I attribute the quarrelsome nature of the Middle Ages young men entirely to the want of the soothing weed. They had no work to do, and could not smoke, and the consequence was they were for ever fighting.

JEROME K JEROME

✪

He was smoking a cigarette with the seriousness of an idler.

G K CHESTERTON

✪

LADY BRACKNELL: Do you smoke?
JACK: Well, yes, I must admit I smoke.
LADY BRACKNELL: I am glad to hear it. A man should always have an occupation of some kind. There are far too many idle men in London as it is.

OSCAR WILDE

George put on a pipe and spread himself over the
easy-chair, and Harris cocked his legs on the table
and lit a cigar.

JEROME K JEROME

TRAMPS

Some few among us bravely struggle to be really free:
they are our tramps and outcasts. We well-behaved
slaves shrink from them, for the wages of freedom in
this world are vermin and starvation.

JEROME K JEROME

✪

The tramp who takes the moon for his candle and
the hedgerow for his couch finds greater joy in his
free life than the stockbroker in his cramped existence. Yet the one is a despised outcast and the other
a venerated citizen, because, forsooth, the vagabond
takes your turnip and the city man your money.

GILBERT QUIN

☞   MONEY
NOBILITY

TRUANCY

While others are filling their memory with a lumber of words, one-half of which they will forget before the week be out, your truant may learn some really useful art: to play the fiddle, to know a good cigar, or to speak with ease and opportunity to all varieties of men.

ROBERT LOUIS STEVENSON

MARK TWAIN

What work I have done I have done it because it has been play. If it had been work I shouldn't have done it.

MARK TWAIN

✪

He hates work more than he hates anything else.

MARK TWAIN ON TOM SAWYER

The young Mark Twain first started writing for his own idle amusement while out prospecting for silver in Nevada in the 1860s, sending humorous pieces to the local newspapers signed 'Josh'. His best characters, like Huckleberry Finn and Tom Sawyer, were always resourceful loafers, who, like Twain himself, distrust the civilising impulse and would rather have lived in the wilds where they could fish and smoke and laze all day and no one could try to educate them or tell them what to do.

Twain continued to write throughout his life in order to maintain the leisurely life to which he had become accustomed since achieving his literary fame. But he refused to become a slave to his art: his favourite place to write was always in bed, and he would regularly receive guests during the day whilst wearing his pyjamas.

THORSTEIN VEBLEN

The life of leisure is beautiful and ennobling in all civilised men's eyes.

THORSTEIN VEBLEN

Thorstein Veblen, the controversial American economist and social critic, wrote an influential thesis entitled *The Theory of the Leisure Class* in 1899. He began by describing the idea of a leisure class – the idle aristocracy at the top of society who shun all degrading work and indulge only in pleasurable pursuits. 'This pervading sense of the indignity of the slightest manual labour is familiar to all civilized peoples,' claimed Veblen. He illustrated this concept with cases from feudal Europe, feudal Japan, Brahmin India, and Polynesia:

'In persons of a delicate sensibility who have long been habituated to gentle manners, the sense of the shamefulness of manual labour may become so strong that, at a critical juncture, it will even set aside the instinct of self-preservation. So, for instance, we are told of certain Polynesian chiefs, who, under the stress of good form, preferred to starve rather than carry their food to their mouths with their own hands.'

Steady on there, chief.

☞   LEISURE
           NOBILITY

WEARINESS

You may be familiar with this snippet from James Boswell's *Life of Johnson*:

BOSWELL: We grow weary when idle.
JOHNSON: That is, sir, because others being busy, we want company; but if we are all idle, there would be no growing weary; we should all entertain one another.

☞   ENERGY

WALT WHITMAN

I loafe and invite my soul,
I lean and loafe at my ease, observing a spear of
summer grass.

WALT WHITMAN

✪

The American poet Whitman
Did little to assist the razor industry
But he erected a plausible philosophy
Of indolence,
Which, without soft concealments,
He called Loafing.

CHRISTOPHER MORLEY

✪

Whitman loafed first and loafed loudest.

WILLARD SPIEGELMAN

Walt Whitman (1819-1892) was indisputably the
greatest of nineteenth-century American poets. In 1840
he wrote a splendid essay in praise of idleness as part of
his series 'The Sun-Down Papers' published in *The Long
Island Democrat*. The following extract is taken from this
essay.

'How I do love a loafer! Of all human beings, none equals your genuine, inbred, unvarying loafer. Now when I say loafer, I mean loafer; not a fellow who is lazy by fits and starts – who today will work his twelve or fourteen hours, and tomorrow doze and idle. I stand up for no such half-way business. Give me your calm, steady, philosophick son of indolence … he belongs to that ancient and honourable fraternity, whom I venerate above all your upstarts, your dandies, and your political oracles.'

In this essay, Whitman imagined a land of loafers – 'some distant isle inhabited altogether by loafers' – devoid of the hurry and bustle of normal life. He finished on a political note:

'For my part, I have had serious thoughts of getting up a regular ticket for President and Congress and Governor and so on, for the loafer community in general. I think we loafers should organise. We want somebody to carry out "our principles". It is my impression, too, that we should poll a pretty strong vote. We number largely in the land.'

Needless to say, like a true loafer, he never quite got it together to run for office.

☞   LITERATURE
         LOAFING

OSCAR WILDE

Hughie Erskine had gone on the Stock Exchange for six months; but what was a butterfly to do amongst bulls and bears? He had been a tea-merchant for a little longer, but had soon tired of pekoe and souchong. Then he had tried selling dry sherry. That did not answer; the sherry was a little too dry. Ultimately he became nothing, a delightful, ineffectual young man with a perfect profile and no profession.

Oscar Wilde

As this extract goes to show, Hughie Erskine, the protagonist in Oscar Wilde's short story 'The Model Millionaire', has a confirmed idle streak. Oscar Wilde's writings are brimming with idle characters – and, like Hughie, they are all are delightful, ineffectual young men with perfect profiles and no professions. Dorian Gray, blessed with eternal youth whilst his portrait grows old and hideous, is undoubtedly an idler. At the beginning we see him 'reclining in a luxurious arm-chair', and he spends the rest of the novel following a path of languid idleness and filthy hedonism. Dorian's companion, Lord Henry Wotton, is an idler too. When we first meet Lord Henry he is lying on a divan of Persian saddle bags, peering at us though thin wreathes of blue smoke from one of his opium-tainted Turkish cigarettes. Lord Henry, Wilde tells us, was always late on principle, his principle being that punctuality is the thief of time. 'What brings you out so early?' Lord Henry's father asks him: 'I though you dandies never got up till two,' he adds, 'and were not visible till five.'

☞   GORING, LORD
        LITERATURE

WISDOM

There seems to be a philosophic contradiction between being busy and being wise. Those who are wise won't be busy, and those who are busy can't be wise. The wisest man is therefore he who loafs most gracefully.

LIN YUTANG

✪

The wisdom of a learned man cometh by opportunity of leisure: and he that hath little business shall become wise. How can he get wisdom that holdeth the plough, and that glorieth in the goad, that driveth oxen, and is occupied in their labours, and whose talk is of bullocks?

ECCLESIASTICUS 38:24-25

With what thought does the wise man retire into idleness? In the knowledge that he will be doing something that will benefit posterity.

SENECA

☞   **INTELLECTUALS**

WORK

Work is a dull thing; you cannot get away from that. The only agreeable existence is one of idleness.

ROSE MACAULAY

✪

I like work; it fascinates me. I can sit and look at it for hours … And I am careful of my work, too. Why, some of the work that I have by me now has been in my possession for years and years, and there isn't a finger mark on it.

JEROME K JEROME

✪

Tennis, which our gallants make a recreation, is much more toilsome than what many others make their work; and yet those delight in one and these detest the other, because we do this out of necessity, and the other out of choice.

ROBERT BOYLE

✪

According to Christian ethics, work is imposed by God on Man as a penance consequent on Original Sin.

CAMILLO BERNERI

Work is the only dirty four-letter word in the language.

ABBIE HOFFMAN

✪

I never forget that work is a curse – which is why I've never made it a habit.

BLAISE CENDRARS

✪

Work consists of whatever a body is obliged to do, and play consists of whatever a body is not obliged to do.

MARK TWAIN

✪

It is impossible to enjoy idling thoroughly unless one has plenty of work to do.

JEROME K JEROME

✪

It is laid as a curse upon men, that they shall live by the sweat of their brows.

MARGARET CAVENDISH

Who first invented Work – and tied the free
And holy-day rejoicing spirit down
To the ever-haunting importunity
Of business, in the green fields, and the town –
To plough – loom – anvil – spade – and, oh, most
sad,
To this dry drudgery of the desk's dead wood?

CHARLES LAMB

✪

Work is the source of nearly all the misery in the
world ... In order to stop suffering we have to stop
working.

BOB BLACK

✪

A strange delusion possesses the working classes of
the nations where capitalist civilisation holds sway ...
This delusion is the love of work, the furious passion
for work, pushed even to the exhaustion of the vital
force of the individual and his progeny. Instead of
opposing this mental aberration, the priests, the
economists and the moralists have cast a sacred halo
over work.

PAUL LAFARGUE

Love of labour is a contradiction in terms.

JEREMY BENTHAM

✪

Work is an activity reserved for the dullard.

HENRY MILLER

✪

Work is just another of man's diseases and prevention is better than cure. If you don't look for work, work won't look for you.

HEATHCOTE WILLIAMS

✪

A great deal of harm is being done in the modern world by a belief in the virtuousness of WORK.

BERTRAND RUSSELL

✪

Only fools work voluntarily; all the rest are bribed or blackmailed. As a rough guide I would say that single people are bribed and married people blackmailed.

S L LOWNDES

Any balanced notion of the good life would suggest that we should work to live, but instead we seem to have created a culture where more of us live to work ... we have created a culture in which work is all important as a source of self-identity to more and more people. Every day, in subtle and insidious ways, we glorify and celebrate a workaholic culture ... Only rarely do we ask whether a work culture that puts people under such unhealthy pressures is sustainable, or indeed desirable.

HELEN WILKINSON

✪

Work expands so as to fill the time available for its completion.

C NORTHCOTE PARKINSON

✪

We live in the age of the overworked, and the under-educated; the age in which people are so industrious that they become absolutely stupid.

OSCAR WILDE

Anybody who works is a fool. I don't work, I merely inflict myself on the public.

ROBERT MORLEY

✪

I loathe all trades. Masters and servants — all — peasants, base.

ARTHUR RIMBAUD

✪

We labour, driven by the whip of necessity, an army of slaves. If we do not work, the whip descends upon us; only the pain we feel in our stomach instead of on our back. And because of that, we call ourselves free men.

JEROME K JEROME

✪

I do not like work even when another person does it.

MARK TWAIN

✪

In capitalist society, work is the cause of all intellectual degeneracy.

PAUL LAFARGUE

Ancient mythologies depict the tiller of the soil as a reprobate paying for his sins of rebellion: Adam, progenitor of the human race, is the angel fallen from the heaven of idleness to the hell of work.

CAMILLO BERNERI

★

Work with some men is as besetting a sin as idleness with others.

SAMUEL BUTLER

☞ DOING NOTHING
IDLENESS
INDOLENCE
LAZINESS
LOAFING

WORKAHOLICS

There are some human beings who assert that they love work and despise indolence. I do not dispute their feelings, but I am bold enough to believe that their inappreciation of idleness is the reward of a life too crowded to permit of the mind comprehending its pleasures.

GILBERT QUIN

✪

If it be difficult to persuade the idle to be busy, it is likewise not easy to convince the busy that it is better to be idle.

SAMUEL JOHNSON

☞   AMBITION
            CAREERISTS
            WORK

THE WORLD

The world is full of willing people. Some willing to work, the rest willing to let them.

ROBERT FROST

✪

Most of the world's troubles seem to come from people who are too busy. If only politicians and scientists were lazier, how much happier we should all be.

EVELYN WAUGH

✪

We have turned the world into a workshop to provide ourselves with toys. To purchase luxury we have sold our ease.

JEROME K JEROME

✪

In this world without quiet corners, there can be no easy escapes … from hullabaloo, from terrible, unquiet fuss.

SALMAN RUSHDIE

☞   CIVILISATION
        MANKIND

YOUTH

It is surely beyond a doubt that people should be a good deal idle in youth.

ROBERT LOUIS STEVENSON

✪

The condition of perfection is idleness: the aim of perfection is youth.

OSCAR WILDE

✪

Young people ought not to be idle. It is very bad for them.

MARGARET THATCHER

✪

'Some one who Must Not be Contradicted said that a man must be a success by the time he's thirty, or never.'
'To have reached thirty,' said Reginald, 'is to have failed in life.'

SAKI

221

The Importance of Being Idle

A young man of eighteen is not in general so earnestly bent on being busy as to resist the solicitations of his friends to do nothing. I was therefore entered at Oxford and have been properly idle ever since.

EDWARD FERRARS IN JANE AUSTEN'S
SENSE AND SENSIBILITY

✪

There is something tragic about the enormous number of young men there are in England at the present moment who start life with perfect profiles, and end by adopting some useless profession.

OSCAR WILDE

The future of our civilisation lies with the young. Young people must be idle. They must be idle because it is very good for them. They must be idle for the sake of mankind. To these young people, I must say this. Your country needs you to do absolutely nothing at all whatsoever. It is your task to resuscitate the tradition of creative laziness before it is too late. Please – for the sake of human civilisation – don't do anything. Be idle. Be as idle as you can.

THE END

INDEX

Aldrich, Nelson W 60
Amasis, king of Egypt 83
Apollodorus 62
Aquinas, Thomas 176
Aristophanes 15
Aristotle 6, 13, 15, 59, 78, 79, 117
Atkinson, Robert 90
Aubrey, John 84
Austen, Jane 222
Ayckbourn, Alan 59, 182

Bagehot, Walter 5, 116, 122, 148
Barrie, J M 199
Bartelby the scrivener (character) 19-20
Bennett, Alan 112
Bentham, Jeremy 214
Berneri, Camillo 211, 217
Bierce, Ambrose 13, 72, 191
Black, Bob 11, 70, 161, 213
Bolt, Robert 143
Boswell, James 106, 205
Boyle, Robert 211
Brooke, Sir Basil Stanlake 24
Brummell, George (Beau) 21
Buchan, Elspeth 25
Buchanan, R 153
Buchanites 25
Buddha 26
Burns, Robert 25
Burroughs, William 198
Burton, Robert 142, 163

Butler, Samuel 115, 217
Byron, George Gordon 32, 154

Calvin, John 156-7
Campbell, John 142
Carlyle, Thomas 36
Cassian, John 175-6
Castlerosse, Lord 60
Cavendish, Margaret 212
Cendrars, Blaise 212
Cervantes, Miguel de 183
Chalmers, Thomas 36
Chang Ch'ao 112
Chapman, George 142
Charles II 169
Chaucer, Geoffrey 93
Chekhov, Anton 55, 78, 130
Chesterfield, Earl of 99
Chesterton, G K 54, 132, 200
Chiltern, Mabel (character) 77
Chiltern, Sir Robert 77
Christie, Agatha 104
Chuang-tse 55, 93
Cioran, E M 56
Clark, Alan 144
Coleridge, Samuel Taylor 45, 183
Collins, Wilkie 52-3
Connolly, Cyril 124
Cook, Eliza 16
Cowper, William 93
Cresswell, D'Arcy 154

de Quincey, Thomas 9
Decius 177
Dell, Floyd 55

Dickens, Charles 52-3, 92, 117
Diogenes 74
Disraeli, Benjamin xiii, 41
Dostoyevsky, Fyodor 186
Downing, Beryl 93

Ecclesiasticus 209
Edgeworth, Miss 27
Edward VI 195
Ehrenreich, Barbara 155
Eichendorff, Joseph von 57-8
Einstein, Albert 96
Emerson, Ralph Waldo 1, 5, 147, 148
Endymion 62
Epitaph of Jas. Albery, The 51
Erskine, Hughie (character) 208

Ferber, Edna 86
Ferrars, Edward (character) 222
Fish, Simon 137
Ford, Henry 69
Foster, Michael 104
Fox, Ruth 102
Francis, Brendan 163
Frost, Robert 220
Fuller, Henry Blake 40
Fuster, Joan 122, 199

George IV 21
Gerhardi, William 116, 173, 199
Giles, Peter 140-1

Goncharov, Ivan 17, 35, 43, 114, 117, 118, 123, 131, 145, 178

Goodchild, Francis (character) 52

Grass, Günter 134

Gray, Dorian (character) 208

Gregory I, St 175, 176

Grocott, Bruce 142

Guérin, Maurice de 102

Guest, Mrs Winston 22

Hall, Bishop 161

Harburg, E Y 187

Harris, Sydney J 80

Hazlitt, William 194

Henry VIII 137, 140, 181, 196

Henry Wotton (character) 208-9

Herodotus 15, 83

Heseltine, Michael 144

Hexter, H J 112, 140-1

Hilton, James 180

Hoffman, Abbie 212

Holland, Vyvyan 31

Homer 127

Horace 90

Howard, Leon 20

Hubbard, Elbert 117

Huizinga, Johann 39

Iannucci, Armando 135

Ichigon Hodan 26

Idle, Thomas (character) 52

Irving, Washington 163, 167-8

James, Henry 9

Jerome, Jerome K 41, 44, 59, 71, 84, 86, 94, 105, 109, 114, 182, 200, 201, 202, 211, 212, 216, 220

Jesus Christ 37

Johnson, Samuel 1, 16, 33, 43, 49, 56, 71, 88, 89, 93, 98, 101, 103, 106, 131, 133, 146, 149, 205, 219

Jonson, Ben 101

Juvenal 82

Keats, John 154

Keene, Donald 107

Kenko Yoshida 13, 26, 84, 107-8, 138, 161

Kropotkin, Peter 34, 63

La Rochefoucauld, François, duc de 88

Lafargue, Paul 15, 108-9, 213, 216

Lamb, Charles 56, 84, 115, 133, 138, 213

Lebowitz, Fran 117, 182, 183

Lessing, Gotthold Ephraim 109

Lewis, C S 114

Liddell, Henry 175

Lin Yutang 4, 9, 16, 39, 41, 100, 113, 119-20, 131, 134, 153, 209

Lombard, Peter 176

Loosemore, W C 191

Lord Caversham (character) 77

Lord Goring (character) 77

Lotus-Eaters 127

Lowndes, S L 148, 214

Macaulay, Rose 211

MacDonald, George 89

Marlowe, Christopher 185

Marquis, Don 98

Maugham, William Somerset 71

Melville, Herman 19-20

Meredith, George 5

Metternich, Prince xiii

Mill, John Stuart xi, 189

Miller, Henry 54, 214

Mitchell, S Weir 94

Montaigne, Michel de 123

Moore, Suzanne 179

Morand, Paul 92

More, Sir Thomas 140-1

Morley, Christopher 126, 206

Morley, Robert 216

Morris, William 155, 187

Munro, H H *see* Saki

Nietzsche, Friedrich 13, 37

Northfield, Wilfrid 191

Oblomov, Ilya Ilyitch (character) 17, 43, 131, 145

Offenbacher, Martin 155

Oglivie, Sir Heneage 27, 100

Ovid 130

Pain, Barry 125

Parkinson, C Northcote 215

Pepys, Samuel 169

Phidias 15

Plato 59

Plutarch 195

Po Chü-I 110

Porter, Cole 179

Powers, Bob 139

Pynchon, Thomas 121

Quin, Gilbert 16, 23, 27, 29, 47, 72, 116, 133, 138, 159-60, 170, 199, 202, 219

Raymond, Walter 28, 88, 116

Reagan, Ronald 80

Repplier, Agnes 40, 87, 102

Rimbaud, Arthur 216

Rip Van Winkle (character) 167-8

Rochester, John Wilmot, 2nd Earl of 169

Rogers, Will 163

Roscoe, Burton 121

Rousseau, Jean Jacques 33, 90, 162

Rowland, Helen 134

Rushdie, Salman 220

Ruskin, John 1

Russell, Bertrand 11, 40, 142, 171, 187, 197, 214

Saki 28, 37, 147, 172-3, 221

Sallust 138

Santayana, George 122

Sawyer, Tom (character) 203-4

Schlegel, Friedrich von 109

Scott, Robert 175

Seneca 102, 166, 174, 210

Seven Sleepers of Ephesus 177

Shaw, George Bernard 70, 153

Shenstone, William 161

Sidney, Algernon 183

Sidney, Sir Philip 46

Skelton, John 181

Slater, Philip 48

Smith, Logan Pearsall 30, 34, 112, 117, 122, 132, 194, 198

Smith, Sydney 54

Socrates 6

Somnus 189

Spiegelman, Willard 206

Stekhel, Wilhelm 94, 166

Stevenson, Robert Louis 36, 78, 81, 87, 89, 92, 115, 190, 203, 221

Sutherland, Douglas 143

Svevo, Italo 121

Tacitus 89

Tennyson, Alfred Tennyson, Baron 115, 127

Thales 75-6

Thatcher, Margaret 221

Theodosius II 177

Thurber, James 73, 126

Tomlin, Lily 35

Trevelyan, G M 49

Trocchi, Alexander 152

Twain, Mark 55, 60, 72, 92, 138, 203-4, 212, 216

Vaneigen, Raoul 115

Veblen, Thorstein 204-5

Virilio, Paul 153

Voltaire xi

Ward, Artemus 63

Watts, Isaac 163, 186

Waugh, Evelyn 48, 175-6, 220

Weber, Max 27, 156

Wesley, John 157

Whitman, Walt 37, 74, 125, 146, 206-7

Wilde, Oscar 56, 77, 88, 100, 101, 130, 198, 200, 208-9, 215, 221, 222

Wilkinson, Helen 215

Williams, Heathcote 103, 214

Wittgenstein, Ludwig 153

Woolf, Virginia 121

Wordsworth, William 98, 154

Yeats, William Butler 154